D1608437

2

An Arcadian Landscape

The California Gardens of A. E. Hanson

1920–1932

Johnson Garden, Montecito, 1928–29.

An Arcadian Landscape

The California Gardens of A. E. Hanson
1920–1932

A. E. Hanson

Edited by David Gebhard and Sheila Lynds
Introduction by David Gebhard

California Architecture and Architects, Number 5
David Gebhard, editor
Hennessey & Ingalls, Inc. Los Angeles 1985

Library of Congress Cataloging in Publication

Hanson, A. E., 1893–
  An Arcadian landscape.

  (California architecture and architects; no. 5)
  Includes index.
  1. Hanson, A. E., 1893–   . 2. Landscape
architecture—California—History. 3. Gardens—
California—Design—History. 4. Landscape architects—
California—Biography. I. Gebhard, David. I. Lynds,
Sheila. III. Title. IV. Title: California gardens of
A. E. Hanson, 1920–1932. V. Series.
SB470.H36A33 1985   712'.092'4[B] 84-29029
ISBN 0-912158-91-3

Copyright © 1985 by A. E. Hanson and David Gebhard
All rights reserved.
Manufactured in the United States of America
Manuscript typed by Jo Ann Merideth
Copy edited by Jean Sedillos
Design and makeup by Murray Rosenthal
Composition by MPC Typographics

The 1978 photographs of the Kirk B. Johnson
garden were taken by Wayne McCall of Santa Barbara.

Published by
Hennessey & Ingalls, Inc.
1254 Santa Monica Mall
Santa Monica, California 90401

Contents

Introduction

by David Gebhard

Overnight palaces and villas seem to spring into being on barren hills and in wooded canyons. Within a short year a garden will blossom where yesterday only greasewood and scrub oak clothed the ground. Wealth and art together have been employed to lay out many of California's gardens. [1]

Though a number of extensive gardens had been laid out in the peninsula below San Francisco and in Southern California before the First World War, it was the decade of the twenties that experienced a renaissance in large-scale private landscape architecture, a renaissance never again equaled in the state. As in the late nineteenth and early twentieth centuries, this renaissance was made possible by the benign climate of coastal California, coupled with the increased availability of water. But there were other ingredients that made the gardens of the twenties unique. The private clients of those years were not necessarily more "cultivated" than those of the previous decades, but were as a group well traveled. They had, in most instances, seen and walked through many of the great and not-so-great gardens of Italy, France, Spain, and England, and even those as distant as Iran and India. And these clients, like their architects and landscape architects, believed in the language of traditional architecture and gardens. The close-to-unanimous wish among the clients of the twenties was to realize in California variations on one or another of the gardens that they had encountered abroad.

The desire to create an instant garden so that it could be experienced at the moment by the original patron was in no way

E. L. Doheny Garden, Beverly Hills, c. 1928. Fountain and garden wall.

unique to California in the twenties. The history of European gardens, especially since the Late Renaissance, is resplendent with examples of large-scale trees and shrubs being moved to a garden; of immense waterworks created to provide for fountains, moving water courses, and pools; and of hills, valleys, and open meadows being created where none existed before. What was to a degree unique in Southern California in the 1920s was that the creation of moderate- to large-scale gardens—the pastime of monarchs and of the landed gentry—was now possible for the upper-middle and middle classes.

To carry out these gardens, there was a need—almost immediately fulfilled—for landscape architects who knew the traditional language of design, were familiar with California's vast horticultural possibilities, and knew how to conduct their profession so that the gardens could all be actually built (as instantaneously as possible and, of course, within the budget).

By the beginning of the twenties in Southern California, a scattering of individuals who had been academically trained in horticulture and landscape design practiced landscape architecture.[2] The great Boston planning and landscape architectural firm of Olmsted and Olmsted had become increasingly involved in Southern California after 1900, especially in their planning and designs for the Palos Verdes Peninsula.[3] The Olmsteds were joined by their Boston colleague, the architect Guy Lowell, author of two of the classic source books for garden and villa design: *Smaller Italian Villas and Farm Houses* (1916) and *More Small Italian Villas and Farm Houses* (1920). Lowell applied his expertise to one of the most complete of the early Mediterranean villas and gardens in California, the Robert G. McGann estate in Montecito (1916).[4]

But most of the practitioners who came to designate themselves as landscape architects followed the path that had prevailed in England since the eighteenth century. They often began their apprenticeship as plantsmen, perhaps working with an established gardener or in a nursery, and then went out to establish their own practices. There were also those like Francis T. Underhill, Lockwood de Forest, and later Elizabeth de Forest, who, like Humphrey Repton or John Loudon in late eighteenth- and early nineteenth-century England, were gentleman or gentlewoman architects/landscape architects.[5] Finally, there were a number of architects who, when they planned smaller grounds and estates, designed them themselves and, in many instances, produced admirable results.

The design of Southern California "Victorian" gardens of the late nineteenth and early twentieth centuries was in essence no different than what one would find in the Northeast or the Midwest. The suburban plot was normally laid out as a miniaturized version of the late-nineteenth-century English picturesque garden; the same was true for California's farms, country houses, and estates. What distinguished a Los Angeles garden from one in the suburbs of Chicago or Boston was the exotic plant material—particularly semitropical trees and plants. No California garden was complete without its specimen araucaria tree accompanied by a sprinkling of palms. The picturesque English landscape tradition of the "natural" garden continued into the thirties and on after the Second World War. In these later picturesque gardens, the imprint of the exotic was minimized, and the native and nonnative trees, shrubs, flowers, ground cover, and lawns were composed to suggest that all was natural. When formal Italian and Spanish gardens became fashionable in the teens and twenties, these gardens were almost always treated as an ordered fragment placed within the artificially created English natural garden.

Winifred Starr Dobyns mentioned in her 1931 volume *California Gardens* that this new Mediterranean renaissance came about

Cochran Garden, Los Angeles, 1928. Garden wall and gate.

when Californians had lost their fear of " . . . the word 'formal' in garden planning."[6] While California gardens of the twenties were highly catholic in their borrowings, the dominant sources were countries bordering the Mediterranean Sea—principally Italy and Spain (both Moorish and Christian). Dobyns and others correctly pointed out that the establishment of the new Mediterranean world on the coast of California relied as much on landscape architecture as it did on architecture. And nowhere was this better fulfilled than in the many courtyard gardens and in the small and large formal gardens created from San Diego north to Santa Barbara.

California's first self-conscious sally into regionalism was the Mission Revival with its ideal of the patio-courtyard bursting forth with semitropical plantings. Though the enclosed patio itself was present in only a handful of Mission Revival buildings, the balanced symmetry (albeit provincial) of the original mission buildings, together with the layout of their cloistered patios, suggested that formalism and reliance on axes were essential to the style. By the early 1900s, the ideal street approach to a suburban Mission villa was via an axial walk and drive; patios, when present, ideally had axial cross walks, balanced planting, and a central posture such as a fountain or pool.[7] Irving J. Gill, who devoted his efforts to abstracting the Mission Revival vocabulary, relied on the formal treatment of the garden to realize his puritanical goals. The principal garden of his classic Dodge house in Los Angeles (1916) projects north from the house with an axis that eventually terminates in a garden structure set into a high wall. In the same house, Gill's outdoor patio off the dining room is a purist synthesis of the classical atrium.[8].

After 1900 the formal garden was increasingly used. Belle

Sumner Angier illustrated and discussed "Italian Gardens," "Enclosed Gardens," and "Terraced Lawns" in her 1906 volume, *The Garden Book of California.*[9] Two years later the San Francisco landscape gardener John McLaren, in his widely read *Gardening in California,* illustrated a plan for a "ten acre tract" that entailed a formal rectangular garden directly adjoining the country villa.[10] And on a much smaller scale, Eugene O. Murmann, in his 1914 *California Gardens,* demonstrated that the picturesque California bungalow set in its small suburban plot was as much at home in the setting of a formal garden as it was in an informal one.[11]

From 1916 on, it was the Santa Barbara architect George Washington Smith who was most fully enamored with the Spanish Andalusian courtyard garden. While the enclosed garden had been employed earlier by Bertram G. Goodhue, Delano and Aldrich, Francis T. Underhill, and others, it was Smith who made the courtyard specifically Spanish. His axial brick, tile, or gravel pathways often traversed by the soft trickle of water in runnels, his central tiled fountains surrounded by potted plants, his elaborate pergolas and masonry seats, and, above all, his use of glazed tile left no question in the visitor's mind that she or he was indeed transplanted into a Hispanic/Moorish world.[12] In Northern California, the architect Clarence Tantu beautifully carried out a similar theme, while in Pasadena the landscape architects Katherine Bashford, Florence Yost, and Lucile Council understood and used the language with perfection.[13]

In Europe the enclosed garden had occurred again and again, and it had assumed many forms. Along with the Hispanic patio and the Italian courtyard, the walled French garden came into popularity in Southern California. In the Southland the walled garden was generally used for confined suburban sites, and as an image it was usually associated with English Tudor or French Norman style.

Lockhart Garden, Los Angeles, 1928. The Playhouse.

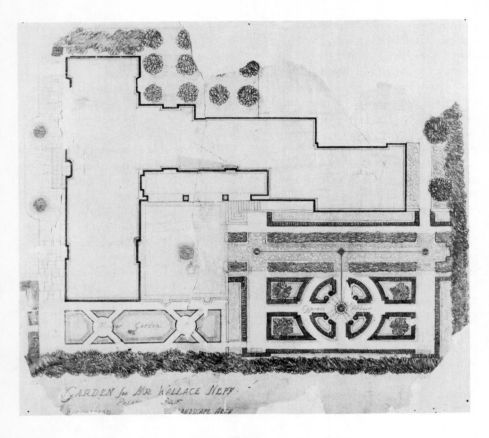

Wallace Neff Garden, San Marino, 1929. Plot plan of the garden.

The walled French garden was principally derived from the sixteenth- through eighteenth-century enclosed gardens associated with the small manor houses in and around Versailles.[14] The California interpretation of this garden type was characterized by a walled, elongated rectangular plot, usually of grass; the end opposite the dwelling being terminated by a pergola, wall fountain, or garden house. Though the geometric precision of the design pointed to France, the general atmosphere of the planting was often quite English.

The first extensive axial garden in Southern California was Waldron Gillespie's great Montecito estate of "El Fureidis," which he, with the advice of Bertram G. Goodhue, began to lay out in 1896. The two friends had traveled to the Mediterranean and on to Persia together, and it was the Islamic garden that most intrigued them.[15] The great axis of "El Fureidis" was defined by cypresses, which led from the principal south terrace down the hillside, continued past the cross pools, and terminated at a classical pavilion. The axis and the garden ended up being more Persian than European. Equally Islamic at "El Fureidis were the many brick-paved paths with their central runnels, which were connected to fountains, basins, and seats. But the purely Spanish and Italian features of the Gillespie house—its interior patio, the pergolated roof terrace, the immense southern terrace with its rectangular pools— were assertive enough to easily convince the viewer that this was a Mediterranean house set in a Mediterranean garden.

The Gillespie garden was followed by an increased number of classical and Mediterranean villas whose gardens were increasingly formal in plan. Before 1920 the most impressive of these were built in and around Pasadena and in Montecito (to the east of Santa Barbara). Though the formal garden came to be associated with regionalism and the Mission Revival, the enthusiasm for this extension of visual control into the landscape was part and parcel of the international Beaux Arts movement. The often illustrated and written about G. W. Wattles garden in Hollywood, designed by Myron Hunt and Elmer Grey (1907-08), with its insistent architecture of tile-covered walls and walkways, revealed how California designers could twist the classical Beaux Arts image so that it appeared Mediterranean, that is, Californian.[16]

By the end of the twenties, the larger gardens contained a set of basic ingredients, and innumerable variations were worked out on these basics. The garden's purpose was to create an illusion that the villa, no matter how small its acreage, was a vast estate set alone in the landscape. With only a few exceptions, the approach to the dwelling was via a serpentine drive, which seemed to wind its way through an informal English garden. In some instances, the rural nature of the site was enhanced by accompanying orchards of olives or citrus. The drive itself would enter a precisely defined (by walls or planting) auto court. Directly opposite the drive entrance to the auto court was the principal facade and entrance to the house. Usually located off the living and/or dining rooms would be a formal axial garden, defined by walkways and paths, planting, and garden features: pools, fountains, pergolas, walls, and garden houses. The defining sides of such axial gardens were usually high, clipped hedges, which often formed separate "garden rooms," with plantings of rose bushes or flowers.

In another direction from the house might be an informal English garden centered on a sloping lawn and defined by an informal curving boundary of shrubbery and trees.

Gardens of this scale were produced throughout the twenties by all of the larger landscape architectural firms. What distinguished the early twenties' gardens from those completed at the end of the decade was the later tendency towards simplicity, accompanied at the same time by more specific references to features derived from historic European gardens, especially to those of Italy rather than those of Spain. It is fascinating to visit these California gardens and to talk with their original owners and landscape architects, for mention will often be made as to how this or that feature was "inspired" by an element found in one or another of the great gardens of the Mediterranean countries. A cascading water course looked back to the gardens of the Villa Lante, or a terraced garden might refer to the Villa Garzoni or to the Villa d'Este.[17]

And what of the bewildering choice of plant material itself? In decided contrast to the specimen approach taken in the late nineteenth century, the designers of the gardens of the twenties used trees, shrubs, and flowers to create the illusion that the garden and its plants were indigenous to the place. Other than a few native species—the California oak, the western sycamore, the bay tree, and the white and red alder—all of these gardens' vegetation was imported. By the end of the decade, the eucalyptus, the palm tree, the acacia, the cork oak seemed as "native" as any oak or sycamore. It did not matter that most of this plant material came from Australia, South America, and southern Africa—its purpose was to enhance the suggestion that Southern California was the Mediterranean coast improved.

Compared to the final decades of the nineteenth century, the designed gardens of the twenties did not express the intensified enthusiasm for individual plants that one associates with the great pre-1900 California horticulturalists. For the landscape architects of the twenties, plants were a means to an end, not an end in themselves. In a good number of these designs—ranging from the small, walled garden to the Hispanic and Italian—the plant material, now adroitly treated as a unified composition, merely served as a backdrop to the architecture of walks, balustraded walls, pools, fountains, and pergolas.

One of the most fascinating accounts and reactions to the gardens of Southern California at the end of the twenties was that of the English gardener and author Marion Crain.[18] Her reactions to these gardens were, as one would

expect, strongly colored by her English experience. She was both intrigued and repelled by the instantaneous nature of these gardens and also by their almost limitless use of semitropical and temperate plant material. She fimly believed that, "More than anything in the world a garden displays personality; the seeing eye walks softly in each new garden it enters, for it is about to discover the owner's very soul. The bias of his mind is there, the range of his ideals, his courage or his slackness under difficulties, his sense of order or disorder, his education, his breed, his tastes, his nature are written in that tract of earth."[19] And what did she see? In Pasadena she breakfasted with Raymond Gould in " . . . a small temple d'amour," situated in a green valley below, " . . . his 'Villa Evarno,' a house of austere and lovely taste in the Florentine manner."[20] In Beverly Hills she

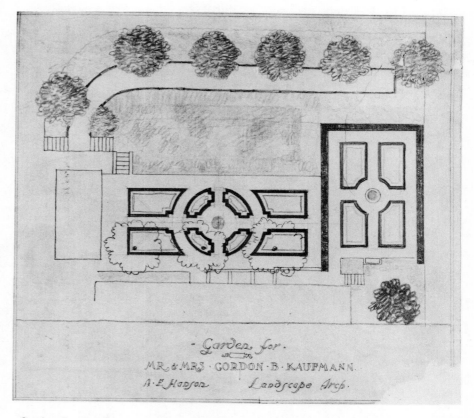

Gordon B. Kaufmann Garden, Holmby Hills, 1928-29. Plot plan of formal gardens next to house.

visited the Ben R. Meyer garden designed by Paul Thiene. Here she found ". . . a big banker's house and garden set on a high hill—very admirably laid out by a man who could afford to buy good taste and had the taste to find it."[21]

"Mary Pickford's garden," Crain remarked, "is like her ringlets were—very pretty and well kept."[22] "I went into Charles Chaplin's garden with a sinking heart; the curly drive was hideously suburban; cement played a loud part in the stone edging; there was the everlasting carpet of blue periwinkle; there was the awful gazania and geranium mixture; there was the familiar blend of plumbago and bridal wreath which custom could never stale to my eye." But finally her tour of the garden was saved by an entire hillside planted in pink ice plant, whose "brave simplicity" represented a "stroke of genius."[23] With A. E. Hanson's design for the Harold Lloyd garden, she was overwhelmed and decidedly uncomfortable. " . . . as one ecstatic female says: 'the Harold Lloyd estate in California is comparable only with the gardens of the Caliphs.' Oh, poor Harold!"[24]

The character of the Harold Lloyd garden and its villa was captured in an article in the December 1931 issue of *Arts and Decoration:* "There is a suggestion of the hills of Fiesole, surrounding Florence, and from that district came inspiration for the imposing house and its magnificent gardens, in the manner of the French Italian Renaissance . . . From the great oak-paneled library, a French door opens to one of the finest vistas of the estate, through the loggia and down an avenue of cyprus trees to a silvery cascade and pool surrounded by pepper trees, and in the far distance the snow-capped peak of San Antonio."[25]

When the gloomy economic aspects of the Great Depression finally took effect at the end of 1931, the creation of great formal gardens all but ceased in California. A few were built during the thirties: the Mrs. W. A. Clark house and garden in Santa Barbara (Reginald D. Johnson, 1933–34) and the Von Romberg house and garden (Lutah Maria Riggs, 1934),

but these were notable exceptions.[26] The more modest approach to gardens that was taken in the 1930s fit in well with the emergence of California's Monterey Revival, which had begun in the mid-twenties. The ideal Monterey Revival garden was essentially a transplanted New England garden with white picket fence, carefully edged and mowed lawn, and accompanying beds of flowers, rose bushes, and climbing flowering vines. Though many of the plants and trees hardly evoked the vegetation of New England, the overall flavor was there.

It is through the sumptuous scene of the 1920s that the landscape architect A. E. Hanson leads us in the narration that follows. His approach to the practice of landscape architecture fits with ease into the Anglo-American landscape tradition. Basically self-taught, educated initially as a plantsman, Hanson was a gifted organizer like such early-nineteenth-century figures as John Claudius Loudon and Joseph Paxton. A person who recognized talent, as is evidenced in his selection of the landscape architect Geraldine Knight Scott and the designer Lee Rombotis, Hanson inspired confidence and respect from architects as well as from his well-traveled clients. Like his clients, he enriched his knowledge of gardens through two extensive trips to Europe, the first in 1927, the latter in 1931. Though we regrettably lack anything approaching a complete record of A. E. Hanson's projected and built gardens, we are fortunate that the records and his memories are able to recreate for us several of his major gardens: that for Harold Lloyd in Beverly Hills (1925–29), the Mrs. Daniel Murphy gardens in Los Angeles (1932), the Henry Kern garden in Holmby Hills (1925), the Kirk Johnson garden in Montecito (1928–1929), and the Archibald Young garden in Pasadena

E. L. Petitfils Garden, Winsor Square, Los Angeles, c. 1928. Plot plan of the garden.

(1929). With the exception of the Young garden, all of these larger gardens were modeled after Italian examples, and they were carried out with knowing taste and reserve. The Young garden, which accompanied an Andalusian house designed by George Washington Smith, illustrates how the provincial atmosphere of southern Spain could be enhanced by a melting together of Moorish and Italian ideas.[27] Of his large-scaled gardens, that for the Kirk Johnson estate (along with its villa by George Washington Smith) represents the culmination of the Italian tradition in California; the Young garden assumes a similar pre-eminence within the state's Hispanic tradition.

When the Great Depression destroyed the market for gardens in California, A. E. Hanson turned his attention to still larger-scaled land use. First he assumed the management of Frank Vanderlip's twelve-acre estate in Palos Verdes Estates (1931–1932); later he established and developed Rolling Hills (1932–1941); following the Second World War he developed the suburban horse-oriented community of Hidden Hills in the western San Fernando Valley.[28] In this expansion of his activities in reorganizing the landscape, he was once again reflecting what had often occurred with Anglo-American landscape architects in the nineteenth century. He was also anticipating the broad planning concerns that have typified the practice of most landscape architects since 1945. By looking at Hanson's gardens of the 1920s, we are experiencing only a fragment, albeit a significant fragment, of this remarkable individual's contributions to the landscape of Southern California. The full impact is apparent when we couple his gardens of the twenties with his activities as a developer during the three decades that followed.

Notes

1. Winifred Starr Dobyns, *California Gardens,* New York: The Macmillan Company, 1931, p. 15.
2. David C. Streatfield, "The Evolution of California Landscape: No. 3, The Great Promoters," *Landscape Architecture,* May, 1977, pp. 229–249; "The Evolution of the California Landscape: No. 4, Suburbia at Its Zenith," *Landscape Architecture,* September, 1977, pp. 417–424. The most prominent landscape architects in Southern California in the 1920s were Charles G. Adams, Wilber D. Cook, Jr., George D. Hall, Ralph D. Cornell, Katherine Bashford, Stephen Child, Lucile Council, Lockwood de Forest, A. E. Hanson, Edward Huntsman-Trout, the Olmsted brothers, Paul Thiene, and Florence Yost.
3. "Millionaire's Colony," *The Architect and Engineer,* vol. 28, August, 1914, p. 121; Frederick Law Olmsted, "Palos Verdes Estates," *Landscape Architecture,* vol. 17, July, 1927, pp. 255–290. The planner Charles H. Cheney was associated with Olmsted and Olmsted in much of their work on the West Coast. See Charles H. Cheney, "Palos Verdes, Eight Years of Development," *The Architect and Engineer,* vol. 100, January, 1930, pp. 35–83. For a recent account of the development of Palos Verdes, see Agusta Fink, *Time and the Terraced Land,* Berkeley: Howell-North Books, 1966.
4. Guy Lowell, *Smaller Italian Villas and Farm Houses,* New York: Architectural Book Publishing Company, 1920.

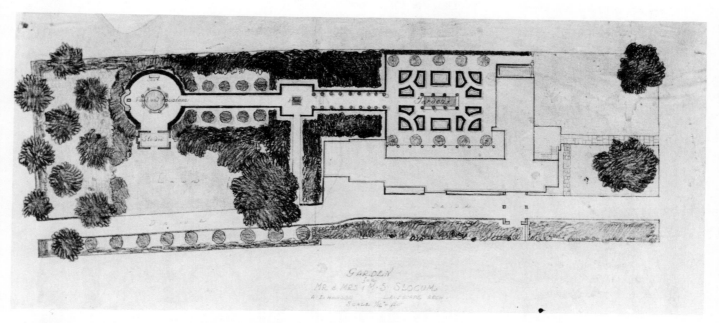

M. S. Slogum Garden, Pasadena, c. 1928. Plot plan of the garden.

5. Several of Francis T. Underhill's and Lockwood de Forest's gardens are illustrated in Winifred Starr Dobyns's *California Gardens*, pls. 11, 12, 44, 72, 115. Underhill's water gardens at "Arcady," the George Owen Knapp estate in Montecito, are illustrated in *Architectural Record*, vol. 45, January, 1919, pp. 66–70. For the work of Lockwood de Forest, see William Peters, *Lockwood de Forest, Jr.*, unpublished M.A. thesis, University of California, Berkeley, 1980.

6. Winifred Starr Dobyns, *California Gardens*, p. 15. The landscape architect and planner Stephen Child observed in his 1927 volume, *Landscape Architecture* (Stanford University Press), ". . . the spirit of cheerfulness and the close connection between art and everyday living which are expressed in the Italian Villagarden makes the Italian treatment appropriate in California," p. 14.

7. For the gardens of the missions, see Victoria Padilla, *Southern California Gardens*, Berkeley and Los Angeles: University of California Press, 1961, pp. 17–35; for Mission Revival gardens see pp. 90–111 in the same volume.

8. For an example of the gardens accompanying the building of Irving J. Gill, see George D. Hall, "The Estate of Mr. W. L. Dodge, Hollywood, California," *The Architect and Engineer*, vol. 61, April, 1920, pp. 87–90. The garden for this house was designed in cooperation with the landscape architect Wilber D. Cook, Jr.

9. Belle Sumner Angier, *The Garden Book of California*, San Francisco: Paul Eldger and Co., 1906, pp. 16, 114.

10. John McLaren, *Gardening in California*, San Francisco: A.M. Robertson, 1908, 1927, pp. 34–35.

11. Eugene O. Murmann, *California Gardens*, Los Angeles: Eugene O. Murmann, 1914, pp. 95–108.

12. David Gebhard, *George Washington Smith 1876–1930. The Spanish Colonial Revival in California*, Santa Barbara: The Art Gallery, University of California, 1964; "George Washington Smith," in Herb Andree and Noel Young, *Santa Barbara Architecture*, Santa Barbara: Capra Press, 1980, pp. 88–93.

13. See Winnifred Starr Dobyns, *California Gardens*, illustration 500.

14. Lewis A. Coffin, Jr.; Henry M. Polhemus; and Addison F. Worthington; *Small French Buildings*, New York: Charles Scribner's Sons, 1921; Philip L. Goodwin and Henry D. Milliken, *French Provincial Architecture*, New York: Charles Scribner's Sons, 1925.

15. Bertram G. Goodhue, "Of Persian Gardens," *Century Magazine*, vol. 73, March, 1907, pp. 739–748; " 'El Fureidis' at Montecito, California, The Villa of James Waldron Gillespie," *House and Garden*, vol. 4, September, 1903, pp. 97–100.

16. Myron Hunt and Elmer Grey, "G. W. Wattles Garden, Hollywood, Calif.," *The American Architect*, vol. 96, September 1, 1909.

17. Harold Donaldson Eberlein, *Villas of Florence and Tuscany*, New York: The Architectural Record Company, 1922; Arthur T. Bolton (editor), *The Gardens of Italy*, with historical and descriptive notes by E. March Phillipps, New York: Charles Scribner's Sons, 1919; J. C. Shepperd and G. A. Jollicoe, *Italian Gardens of the Renaissance*, London: Ernest Benn, 1925; H. Inigo Triggs, *The Art of Garden Design in Italy* (2 vols.), London: Longmans, Green and Company, 1906; Edith Wharton, *Italian Villas and Their Gardens*, with pictures by Maxfield Parrish, New York: Century, 1903 and 1904.

18. Marion Crain, *Gardens in America*, New York: Macmillan, 1932.

19. Ibid., p. 130.

20. Ibid., pp. 124, 126.

21. Ibid., p. 137. The site plan of "La Collina," the Ben R. Meyer estate off of Doheny Drive in Beverly Hills, was illustrated in *California Southland*, vol. 7, no. 63, March, 1925, p. 26; Paul G. Thiene, "Water Features: Notes on Experience in California Gardens," *Landscape Architecture*, vol. 17, October, 1927, pp. 43–51.

22. Ibid., p. 134.

23. Ibid., p. 136.

24. Ibid., p. 137.

25. "Italian Garden on the Pacific Slopes," *Arts and Decoration*, vol. 36, December, 1931, pp. 56–58. See also Elmer T. Peterson, "Harold Lloyd in His Garden," *Better Homes and Gardens*, vol. 7, September, 1928, pp. 20–21, 66–67.

26. Lutah Maria Rigg's villa for Von Romberg is illustrated in Herb Andree and Noel Young, *Santa Barbara Architecture*, Santa Barbara: Capra Press, 1980, pp. 194–195; for Edward Huntsman-Trout, see Lynn Bryant, "Edward Huntsman-Trout, Landscape Architect," *Review*, Society of Architectural Historians, Southern California Chapter, vol. 2, no. 1, Winter, 1983, pp. 1–6.

27. Marion Brownfield, "The Spanish Influence in the Gardens of Southern California," *Garden and Home Builder*, vol. 32, December, 1920, pp. 186–188; Winchton L. Risley, "An Inner Garden from Old Spain," *California Home Owner*, vol. 5, August, 1927, pp. 7, 27. The two best summations of California's Spanish gardens of the 1920s are to be found in Margaret Atchley, *California Homes and Gardens*, Los Angeles: Margaret Atchley, 1931; and in Winifred Starr Dobyns's *California Gardens*. A number of the Santa Barbara and Montecito gardens are discussed and illustrated in Ervanna Bowen Bissell, *Glimpses of Santa Barbara and Montecito Gardens*, Santa Barbara: The Schauer Printing Company, 1926; Warner Lincoln Marsh, "Landscaping the Spanish House," *Sunset*, vol. 64, January, 1930, pp. 18–19.

28. Aspects of A. E. Hanson's work at Palos Verdes and later at Rolling Hills are contained in his volume, *Rolling Hills, The Early Years*, Rolling Hills: City of Rolling Hills, 1978.

Autobiographical Notes

Early Days

I was born December 20, 1893, in Chino, a suburb of Ontario, California. My father, who had come to Ontario from Canada in 1885, was a land developer, specializing in the planting of orange groves for sale in five- to ten-acre parcels. He also had a nursery in Ontario for the sale of ornamental plants. The majority of his buyers were prosperous retirees from the Middle West, who came to Southern California in the 1880s. The skies were always blue, the air was always pure, and Southern California was a paradise where people had never heard of pollution or smog.

In 1889, my maternal grandparents, Mr. and Mrs. Edward Parker (He was a retired manufacturer of buggies and surreys), came to Ontario from Cincinnati, Ohio, with their two daughters, who were then in their early twenties. The older was Charlotte Parker. She had studied art in Cincinnati and had become proficient in painting miniature portraits on ivory.

The Parker family bought a ten-acre orange grove from my father, and he and Charlotte Parker were married a couple of years later.

My earliest recollection is following behind the Mexican ranch hand as he irrigated the young orchard next to our house. How good the warm earth felt to my bare feet. I was fascinated with the

A. E. Hanson, 1927.

slow flow of the water down the irrigation ditch. How pleasant life was in those days; how wonderful the view of snowcapped Mt. Baldy; how blue the sky, how fresh the air—what fun it was to be alive!

My next memory is my first day at kindergarten in the Seventeenth Street School, Los Angeles. On my graduation from grammar school, I attended old Los Angeles High on Hill Street. The location is now the intersection of Hill and the Santa Ana Freeway.

I went to high school for two years. The second year I studied, among other subjects, geometry, zoology, and botany. I had always loved the outdoors, plants, and birds.

The geometry teacher introduced me to an important truth. She told her class not to try to remember formulas, not to try to remember that "the square of the hypotenuse of a right triangle is equal to the sum of the square of the other two sides," but to learn where to find that information. That I've never forgotten.

At the end of that school year, it was necessary for me to go to work to help support the family. My father was away a great deal on business, and my mother had to raise three of us—an older brother, a younger sister, and me.

For a number of years I had had a *Saturday Evening Post* route, and I also sold the *Saturday Evening Post* at Fourth and Spring Streets in downtown Los Angeles. At that time the *Saturday Evening Post* was the leading weekly periodical. Nearly all of the foremost authors had their stories serialized in it. I won many competitions by selling the greatest number of *Posts* in the western United States. I learned salesmanship.

One year after I dropped out of high school, I took a job in British Columbia working for a corporation that bought large blocks of forest acreage suitable for apple orchards. They cut off the pine and

fir trees, pulled out the stumps, then planted young apple trees and sold the developed land in blocks of twenty-five acres or more.

The corporation, in a broad sense, was a type of landscape architecture firm. It laid out a township with a small community center composed of a general store, boarding house, post office, and other buildings. It put in roads and brought in water. The apple orchards depended on irrigation, because there was not enough rainfall. The water was brought several miles by damming up a creek and forcing the water into a square wooden flume, three feet wide and three feet high, open at the top.

So I learned one facet of landscape architecture: the processing of land from a virgin forest to a small town and a surrounding agricultural community. I learned firsthand about laying out roads, laying out a town site, plotting blocks of acreage for fruit groves, and all of the other necessities to make a community. This facet of landscape architecture didn't involve laying out gardens or estates for affluent clients. But what I learned and observed in British Columbia was invaluable to me when I later was to create the communities of Rolling Hills and Hidden Hills in the environs of Los Angeles.

I worked six days a week, ten hours a day. It was hard but fascinating work. The men I worked with were tough lumberjacks. Our housing was tents, four men to a tent.

Sundays I played the Gramophone and washed my clothes, heating the water in a round, galvanized tub over wood that I had split myself. For relaxation on Sunday afternoons, I would go to a log fallen across the creek, drop in a line baited with a grub or a worm, and catch magnificent trout. The water in the creek was ice cold; the fish meat was firm and

sweet. What a life that was for a teen-aged city boy from Southern California!

But all good things must end. In August 1914 Kaiser Wilhelm II decided that he would twist the British Lion's tail and become emperor of the world. With the start of World War I, all of the company's operations shut down, and I was out of a job.

On my return to Los Angeles, my mother, my brother, and my sister were delighted to see me. My father's business had collapsed, and he was in the East looking for new opportunities. My mother had the burden of raising the family. I was then twenty-three years old; my brother was twenty-five; my sister, sixteen. My brother and I had to work.

I, an immature youngster, did not realize how much I had learned about land planning (landscape architecture). I was undisciplined in the sense that I had never learned to study or perform routine tasks. I had very little book learning. I hated the indoors—I loved the outdoors. What could I do? The family needed money.

I had heard of Theodore Payne, a seed collector and grower of native California flora. He was also a thoroughly trained English gardener. He had come to Southern California and been employed by the great Polish tragedienne Madame Modjeska, who had acquired an isolated spot in El Dorado Canyon near Santa Ana so that she would have a spot of wilderness in which to recuperate from her strenuous worldwide tours. Theodore Payne eventually went into the seed and nursery business, specializing in native plants and shrubs.

I called on Mr. Payne at his seed store and told him that I had just come down from British Columbia. I told him what I had been doing there and that I would very much like to work for him and learn about collecting seeds and raising plants. He gave me a job in his nursery.

I worked in the nursery five days a week, ten hours a day, and on Saturdays worked in the downtown store located on the west side of Main Street, between Third and Fourth. I got there early Saturday morning, swept out the store, did odd jobs, and waited on the customers when Mr. Payne and his assistant Mr. Whelton were busy. The hours flew by.

I played a game with myself by trying to sell a package of baby blue-eye seeds, a California wild flower, to every customer I waited on. When I had finished putting up the merchandise the customer wanted, I told him about the baby blue-eyes, and how nice they would be in his garden. I picked up a package of seeds and deliberately thrust it at him so that he had to take it or let it drop. When he took it, he mentally became the possessor of that package of seed, and nine times out of ten I completed the sale. I guess I learned the value of strong salesmanship early in my career.

When we closed the store at ten o'clock Saturday night, after I had put in a day beginning at seven-thirty in the morning, I would walk around the block to the Saddleback Restaurant, which backed up to our seed store, and sit up front at the long counter where the chefs were grilling the most delicious food. And I would squander some of my pay on T-bone steak, medium rare, thick French-fried pototoes, and onion rings. It was customary to tip the chefs five or ten cents. After awhile, people got to calling me "T-bone."

Monday morning I was at the nursery by 7:30. There were just two employees—the nurseryman and the man of all work—me. I learned a tremendous amount. Theodore Payne had found the secret of growing Matilija poppy

plants from seeds. He had observed that after a brush or forest fire, following the next season's rains, the wild flowers and shrubs sprang up in great profusion, and he reasoned that this came about because the fire's heat, together with the lye in the remaining ashes, softened the seed shells so that they could germinate. He could raise Matilija poppies from seeds when no one else could, and naturally he did not divulge his secret—nor did we, his employees.

I loved learning about growing plants. We mixed sand and soil—and a certain amount of street sweepings, peat, oak leaves—which made the finest kind of seed-flat soil. I learned how to sow seeds in a flat, how to give them the right amount of water, when to take them out of the lath house and put them in the sun, how to put the seedlings into a two-inch pot, then move them on to a three-inch, a four-inch, and a six-inch pot. I was getting a tremendous amount of experience and was unconsciously learning a trade.

I think when you are a youngster, you learn a tremendous amount if you are interested in your work. You almost absorb it through your pores. Years later, when I became a landscape architect, no plant supplier was foolish enough to try to sell me a pot-bound plant.

The nursery was composed of two corner lots across the street from each other. After the plants had been raised to a certain size, they were taken across the street to the other lot. We used old-fashioned wheelbarrows, which are now antiques. They were all wood, except the wheel, which had an iron rim. The sides were removable and could be lifted off so you could put on a wider load if you wanted. It wasn't hard to push the wheelbarrow down from the curb and across the street, but I always had a terrific struggle to get the wheel up the curb. I would

push down on the handles with all my might to raise the wheel up, and then shove as hard as I could. It took a lot of effort.

One day, at this critical stage, the colored street sweeper came along. These sweepers are now extinct. He had a pushbroom and a barrel slung between two wheels. There were lots of horses on the streets, so he had lots of work. Just at the point when I was struggling manfully, using the language I had learned from the loggers in British Columbia, he said, "Boy, stop! Use your head!"

He grabbed hold of the two handles of the wheelbarrow, turned it around so that he stood above the street on the curb, and very gently pulled the wheelbarrow to him. The wheel rolled up the curb just as easy as cutting butter.

He said, "Boy, see! There's always an easy way and a hard way. Do it the easy way and you won't be near so tired at the end of the day."

There are lots of lessons that are not written about in books.

The highlight of working for Theodore Payne was going on a seed-collecting trip. We would take the train out to a place where Payne knew certain varieties of wild flowers grew. He would hire a one-horse buggy, and we would drive across the desert, or across the San Fernando Valley, collecting seeds of all the different kinds of native California wild flowers.

We would come to a patch of purple lupine, spread our canvas on the ground underneath the plant, and shake the seeds onto it. The trick was to find patches that did not contain other wild flowers, so that you could gather one variety at a time. This was not forced labor as far as I was concerned—it was a picnic! I could eat a mammoth lunch, and if it was an overnight trip, I could eat supper until the cows came home. Payne paid the bill, of course, but I was a bargain. He didn't mind.

Working in a lath house is very sleep inducing. You have the warm earth, the wetting down of the plants, which causes a lot of humidity; then you have the constant flickering shadow produced by the lath. I would eat my lunch sandwiches and start to read a book, and the next thing I knew, the nurseryman was saying, "Wake up. It's time to work."

Meanwhile, big events were shaping up in 1915. The Panama Canal was due for completion. San Francisco and San Diego were to have a World's Fair, opening in the spring of 1915. Los Angeles was not the romantic spot that these two cities were. There was nothing very picturesque about our man-made harbor. Los Angeles was pretty much sweaty money—although we did have civic pride. One of the ways that Los Angeles celebrated the opening of the Panama Canal was to plant gardens on the west side of Figueroa Street. This frontage was part of Exposition Park.

Four firms were asked to put in model landscaping, each one to plant its plot in the nursery stock for which it was well known. Theodore Payne, of course, wanted to duplicate the native California landscape, and this we did.

He told the two of us at the nursery exactly what he wanted and sent us over to the plot. The first morning we started grading, raking, smoothing, and starting to plant the native shrubs in precise, orderly rows. Late in the afternoon on the first day, Theodore Payne came along, and when he saw what we were doing, he was furious.

"You people!" he said. "You've both been with me out in the country collecting seeds and plants. Did you ever see them grow in rows? Did you ever see more than six square feet flat? We want to reproduce a piece of native land-scape."

He grabbed the dozen short stakes I held in my hand, which I was going to use to spot where I wanted to plant native palm trees, and he threw them—broadcast them—and said, "That's the way Mother Nature plants palm trees!"

And that was another lesson I learned about landscaping that was not found in a textbook. When we finished our plot, under Mr. Payne's watchful eye, it did resemble a piece of native landscape.

For my vacation during the summer of 1915, I went, with two neighborhood boys, to the San Francisco World's Fair. The cheapest way to go was by steamer. As we steamed out of the San Pedro Harbor, passing the Palos Verdes Hills, I never dreamed that someday I would build a community there.

Steaming into San Francisco through the Golden Gate, we were three of the most seasick, unhungry boys that you could imagine. The San Francisco World's Fair, next to the Presidio, was something out of this world to us. In the more than half century since then, I have never failed on a visit to San Francisco, to revisit the Palace of Fine Arts, with its magnificent setting and its beautiful lagoon in the foreground. In 1915 I knew nothing about architecture, but the monumental size, the beautiful design, and the execution thrilled me. The scale of the Palace of Fine Arts was something completely unfamiliar to me. Why can't we have more of that kind of architecture—something to give the public a lift of heart?

Next I went alone to the San Diego Fair, and I walked on clouds for one solid week. The setting in the hills, just a stone's throw from downtown San Diego, was and still is absolutely superb. From the minute I approached the arroyo and saw that magnificent bridge with its curving arch, I was hooked

on architecture! I crossed that high bridge and on the left came to the replica of a Spanish-American cathedral. And across the street a replica of the Municipal Palace in some South American city had been built. I had never before heard the name Bertram Goodhue, but I never forgot it after that. Bertram Goodhue had produced, in my opinion, a classic piece of architecture.

Not so many years ago I took two of my grandsons to the Fair, and I was uplifted just as I was that first day some fifty years earlier.

The gardens at the San Diego Fair also impressed me deeply. You went down the main street, and on either side were beautiful colonial buildings connected with an arcade. The various buildings along the arcade were separated from each other by small formal gardens. One garden led to another, but rarely did you see more than one at a time—the visitor was constantly surprised and delighted.

When I returned to Los Angeles, I knew what I was going to be—a landscape architect. Two days after I returned, I called on Paul J. Howard, the most prestigious man in the landscape business of that day. He had the "carriage trade." I told him that I had worked a year for Theodore Payne, but I wanted to become a landscape architect, that I wanted to work for him because in my eyes he was better than anyone else in California.

I sold myself to Mr. Howard and started out as an errand boy who did all the odd jobs no one else wanted. However, every time I could find an excuse, I went to the drafting room. The head draftsman and designer was a man named Zimmerman; he had been trained in Germany and held a master's degree in landscape design. Zimmerman's work fascinated me. Then a sad thing happened. Paul Howard found that I could sell, and he put me out "chasing" jobs by contacting residential architects and people who were building new houses.

There was, in the early 1900s, a weekly magazine called *The Southwestern Contractor*. Every issue had the news of all construction work, from sewer lines to office buildings, factories to residences. It carried news items as to what every architect was doing. It also printed all the building permits, showing the costs of each job. While working for Paul Howard, I learned a great deal about construction in Los Angeles.

Paul Howard was not actually in the nursery business, as were his brothers in the firm of Howard & Smith, but he did render a service to his clients by recommending replacements for shrubs and selling clients Dutch bulbs for their gardens every fall. I would go to all the clients with a catalog of the latest imports from Holland, and I did get to see many of the fine gardens of the time in Los Angeles and Pasadena. I was a good salesman, but selling was not what I wanted to do.

I put in almost a year with Paul Howard and then decided that if I could sell for him, I could sell for myself as well. I also believed that I, too, could design and build gardens.

I had to start from absolute scratch. I became a landscape contractor, planting very small places, competing against the Japanese. I learned a lot about overhead, costs, and risks of contracting.

And then Woodrow Wilson, "to make the world safe for democracy," declared war on Germany on April 6, 1917. The handwriting was on the wall for all boys of my age.

In the fall of 1917, I enlisted in the 144th Field Artillery—"The California Grizzlies." After train-

ing at Camp Kearney, I was offered a job as landscape gardener at the camp. That wasn't my idea of saving the world for democracy, so I volunteered for overseas service. A few weeks later we landed in France, and I was plunged into the front lines.

World War I was a shattering experience for all the young men who fought in it; I was no exception. Nightmare gas attacks, emaciated and exhausted horses, deafening artillery. All that and more. But on the morning of November 11, 1918, armistice was declared. The fighting was over, and I had survived.

One good thing came out of the war for me. After the armistice, while still in the army, I was able to do some sightseeing in France and England. I saw many sights that were to deepen my appreciation of natural beauty and of man's ability to enhance it.

I was in Paris Easter Sunday, 1919, and, although not a Catholic, I attended eleven o'clock mass at Notre Dame Cathedral. It was packed with people. Practically every Frenchman had lost either an arm or a leg, or had been severely wounded. Their chests were covered with medals.

That afternoon I saw the gardens of the Tuileries and visited Napoleon's Tomb. The French certainly are past masters of theatrical staging. And the sights that Easter Sunday afternoon—after the armistice—were unforgettable.

My division was assigned to the Army of Occupation in Germany. In April 1919 I was fortunate enough to be granted a two-week pass to visit England. I obtained the leave for England because I had a letter of introduction to a great-aunt of mine.

I boarded the troop ship for England at Calais. After my arrival in England, I did my duty: visited my aunt and obtained proof

that I had visited her. Then I was on my own for ten perfect days.

The first two days I spent at Kew Gardens, and that was a liberal education for a landscape architect-to-be. I ran into a young girl dusting a plant with a camel hair brush and asked her why. She said, "Don't you know, this is a very rare plant. It's a *Fremontia*. It comes all the way from Southern California."

I told her that I came from Southern California and that the plant was a native—just a part of our chapparal—and that I had once spent days gathering its seeds. So from then on, we were kindred souls.

I visited one private garden after another. I don't believe that any nationality loves gardens the way the English do. The weather is superb for flowers.

The forgotten 4th Division was replaced in September 1919. It took us seventeen days to sail from Brest to the United States of America. Our cattleboat was so crowded with men that we were only allowed four hours a day on deck, and we were all seasick until we passed the Statue of Liberty, New York Harbor. The next day we left for San Francisco, to be discharged at the Presidio.

As soon as I was discharged, I returned to Los Angeles. I had my discharge pay and little money besides. I was one of the great unwashed—a GI bum, one more unemployed. I decided to pick up where I had left off. I would resume landscaping.

Becoming a Landscape Architect

For the first year after the war, I did landscape contracting. I was a landscape gardener, defined as one who is skilled in the art or work of placing or arranging lawns, trees, bushes, etc. on a plot of ground to make it more attractive. I did small jobs, that really consisted of planting lawns and shrubbery around the base of a house for a fixed price.

After my first year back in Los Angeles, Frances A. McVay and I were married on September 26, 1920. We had lived on the same street in Los Angeles and had known each other since she was five years old and I was seven. Later she had gone east to college at Wellesley. Because of the continuing close relationship between our families, our friendship was reestablished when she returned to Los Angeles.

When I went into business for myself, I contacted all the architects who specialized in residential work. I made up a sales kit of photographs of the gardens that I had done and would leave the photograph album, of which I had a number of copies made, with the architect for him to look over at his leisure. I would also contact the owners of the new houses and leave an album of my work with them.

In other words, I put on an active sales campaign. To be able to sell is very important. What is the use of having a lot of ideas, painting a lot of pictures, being able to sing if nobody will look at your art or listen to your songs?

In two years I was well enough established so that I determined to go after larger commissions. I would call myself a landscape architect. I would do landscape architecture, which, again according to the dictionary, is the art of changing the natural scenery of a place to produce the most attractive or desirable effect.

I would apply all that I had learned working for Paul Howard and all that had rubbed off on me by watching his head designer lay out estates. I would go to night school and take architectural drawing. But after two weeks of evening classes at old Polytechnic High School, at Washington and

Figueroa, I found out that I could hire the teacher, who, in the daytime, was a practicing architect.

And that set the pattern for the future. Why should I try to do something that I was unskilled at when it was easy to hire a skilled person to do the job? And that principle I followed all the rest of my business career. I would be the orchestra leader. I would direct. I did not have to know how to play every instrument or any instrument in the orchestra. All I had to do was to choose good men, read the score, and direct them.

Salesmanship

I was the salesman, but to sell I had to have a product. The product was the drawings, or renderings, or models—something to show the client the kind of garden I was talking about.

By 1922 I had done a lot of work. I had built a lot of gardens, and I had many satisfied clients— or, to use a more down-to-earth word, customers. They, in turn, would recommend me or in some cases make an appointment for me with a friend of theirs who needed a landscape architect. From there on, it was up to me.

I would meet with Mr. and Mrs. Smith. I would listen, which is a hard job for me to do. I listened to what they had in mind for their garden. I would also find out how many children they had and their ages, and whether they had dogs. I would size up the furniture in the Smiths' home to try to determine their living style. I'd find out what their religion was and in general try to learn all I possibly could about them. Then I would try, mentally, to step into their shoes and to visualize the kind of garden I would like to have if I were in their place.

Then I would go back to the office, sit down with my designer, and try to communicate to him the

kind of people the new clients were, the kind of garden I thought they should have, and how much I thought they would be able and willing to spend on it. I would make some hen-scratchings on a piece of paper of some ideas I thought would please them. Then it was up to him.

As my business prospered, I could hire the finest designers. I could pay them more money than anyone else. The head designer would make a colored sketch of the garden—not in great detail, just something I could take back to the clients to see if that rendering was more or less what they had in mind. I would tell them of the merits of doing it that way and give them some idea about the cost.

In many cases it was not necessary for the clients to come to the office. I could take the drawings and the renderings to their home to talk to them—many times it would be in the evening when both the man and the wife were available. But for an expensive job, we would build a model, and then the clients would have to come to the office.

Everything about the office was salesmanship, from the moment the client opened the door. He was greeted by my receptionist, a very pleasant, smiling person with a nice voice. Renderings of gardens we had made and two etchings of ancient gardens were displayed on the reception-room wall. Then the client would be shown into my office, which had a large table and some comfortable chairs. The walls were lined with books on landscape architecture. One wall had on it some renderings of outstanding gardens we had made.

For many of the gardens from 1927 on, we made Plasticene models of the gardens. It was a very realistic way of showing the clients what their garden would look like. I rigged up a revolving piano stool and placed the model on it, high enough so that it would be at the clients' eye level when they were seated. Then I would ask them to look through a powerful reading glass down the paths of the garden. In that way they could actually see what that garden was going to look like and feel they were really in the garden. They had all the illusion of the garden in full scale, and, because the model was on the revolving piano stool, they could see different parts of the model without moving their chairs.

Of course I didn't get every garden job I went after. I made it a practice never to take clients if I didn't think I could get along with them. If I thought they didn't like the way I talked, or my necktie, or my voice, I wouldn't take them. It takes ten satisfied clients to overcome the unfavorable publicity from one dissatisfied client. Never take a job unless you can get along with the people. I was fortunate that from 1927 on, I had more work offered me than I could possibly handle; I could pick and choose the kind of garden I wanted to do, and I could be very fussy about taking on a client.

As soon as a client had okayed the plan—the layout and the budget—we went to work full blast. We never let up on the job; we never quit. We would go as fast and as hard as we possibly could. Do the job while they're interested; do it while they're enthusiastic. Don't ever let it get stale. People can sneer at salesmanship, but without salesmanship things would not be built.

And now we come to the most important part of doing creative work: getting the opportunity to do it. You can have all the ideas in the world—they can be superb—but they're no good unless you've got a client, and in the case of landscape architecture, the client has to be Mr. Moneybags.

Landscape architecture—the creation of gardens—garden architecture—is one of the greatest of luxuries. People will build a fine home. They'll employ a very talented architect. They'll have a superb piece of land. They'll retain a top-notch interior decorator. And then, nine times out of ten, they become tired of spending money, and landscape architecture becomes a stepchild. It is something they can easily get along without. They can get a garden contractor to put in some shrubs and a lawn. So, how do you go about getting the job, if you're a landscape architect?

If it's a new house, and you are friendly with the architect, he can introduce you to the client. Or, you can go to the owner directly to see if you can sell your talents. If it's a remodeling job, and the people want to redo the landscaping, you can contact them either through the architect or by tracking down the building permit.

If, on the other hand, the house is not being remodeled, but the client wants to redo his garden, the only way you're going to get a contact with that prospective client is by having someone recommend you. The best recommendation, of course, comes from a satisfied customer. Such a customer is the best sales tool of all.

Garden Design

By 1922 a definite pattern was beginning to emerge in my work. Most of the gardens were city back yards, not in any derogatory sense, simply that they were yards at the back of the house. Most of them weren't more than 60 feet wide by 120 feet deep—maybe smaller.

The house usually had a terrace or a porch in the rear. From there you could look to the rear lot line, where I would place something of interest—a pergola, a teahouse, a gazebo, a birdbath, or something else that would draw your eye from the porch back to the back property line. That was a terminal to which your eye was drawn, giving the garden focus.

We would heavily screen the sides and the back property line so that the owners, sitting on the porch, could have complete privacy. But then, to add interest, there would be some sort of a little garden tucked away on one side that wasn't seen until you walked halfway from the porch to the back terminal. This added interest to the whole area.

If you can imagine one tremendously big room, all open, in which you see everything at once—you can see it doesn't have too much interest. But if you take this large, uninteresting room and break it up into several rooms, it is more livable and enjoyable; it has some surprises. The same idea applies to a garden.

I'll try to illustrate it in another way. Imagine a theater stage with you in the audience, in front of the orchestra, looking beyond the footlights at all the scenery. It seems a good distance to the back of the stage. But this is an illusion; there is actually very little distance between the footlights and the back of the stage—probably not more than sixty feet.

Over the centuries theater people have become expert in creating this illusion of tremendous distance with props, stage settings, and scenery. This is what I was trying to do in gardens, trying to create an illusion. It was very important in the small gardens at the rear of the house. It's always necessary to have a terminal point, something that draws the eye to that point. But interrupting the distance, without obscuring the view, adds depth.

Let me give you a very simple example. Draw a straight line, six inches long. Draw another line. The second line should not be a continuous line, but should be drawn for an inch then broken, and so on, until it is six inches in length. This broken line can be drawn either above or below the solid line—it makes no difference. Now look at the two lines. Your eye will pass over the unbroken line rapidly. Now compare that time with how long you spend looking at the broken line. Your eye travels over the first inch to the empty space. Your mind and your eye stop for approximately one second. Then your eye picks up the next inch, then comes to another empty space, stops, and then jumps a space. It takes longer to look at a broken line, and that's what I tried to do in my gardens, especially in the small city back yards. Even though they were small, when you were in one of them, after the plants had grown for a couple of years, you were not conscious of being in a throbbing, confusing city. To be fanciful, you were in a little Garden of Eden.

I did maybe three or four hundred of these gardens—city gardens—during the time I was in the landscaping business—using the same theory for all. Years after I had given up the practice of landscaping, I came across a fascinating book written by a very scholarly man, Edward S. Morse, director of the Peabody Academy of Science: *Japanese Homes and Their Surroundings* (1886). Having spent some time in Japan, Morse goes into minute detail as to how the Japanese gardens were built. It interested me that the Japanese were creating gardens in the heart of Tokyo, a very congested city, at the same time I was building city gardens in Los Angeles. In both cases the gardens were designed for people of means, to give them a little spot of nature to come to, a few plants, a place to relax, a place of tranquility.

Much earlier I had discovered another book about small gardens in Versailles, which had talked about the same purpose for a garden. Whether it's Japan,

whether it's Los Angeles, whether it's Versailles—people are all trying to escape. They're trying to get into a little bit of paradise all their own—a little Garden of Eden where they'll have privacy and quiet. Of course, only the very, very wealthy can buy enough land to really escape from the noise and the confusion and the density of people.

But from the design point of view, the size of the garden has nothing to do with how good a retreat it is. With the right technique and design, even a small back yard can be made into at least a partial escape from the pressures of the city.

Organization

At first, all I needed in the way of an organization were three good foremen and a crew of competent workmen. I had the plan for the garden made by an architect who was willing to work in the evening to earn extra money.

There were three elements in the making of these small gardens: grading and sowing, sprinkling, and planting shrubs. By grading, I mean raking smooth to get the lawn to slope as we wished, not grading in the way of Caterpillars or tractors. Remember, these were all city lots. I found, by trial and error, a man, Elmer Dilts, who had the knack of grading a lawn. Elmer Dilts worked for me for years. He had the gift of being able to take a rake and shovel and really do a job of grading. He was an expert.

Next I found a sprinkler contractor with whom I could work, who was good, and whose prices were not exorbitant. He would make the layout for the sprinkling system and install it.

Then I found a man who was good at planting shrubs. He was German; he was an old crab; he

was hard to get along with, but he certainly knew his business, and he worked for me for years.

So we had, to start with, someone who could make the drawings of the garden, someone who could grade the garden, someone who could install the sprinkling system, and someone to handle the shrubs. Very elementary, but the first steps.

As the work continued, I got acquainted with a number of men who had their own small trucks and could haul debris from the various jobs and supply topsoil.

In doing the Harry Calendar job in Windsor Square, which had been an oil field, with the ground containing some tar and a great deal of hardpan, I found it necessary to dynamite the holes for the plants. I got hold of an organization that made a specialty of this and obtained a permit to dynamite. One more cog in our wheel.

Then, when I got more jobs than I could handle—more than I could supervise alone—I got hold of a good carpenter foreman to be my assistant. He could handle three or four jobs at a time.

I found a land-surveying firm— that is, civil engineers—who were cogenial and with whom I could get along. Another element was added to my organization.

My architectural department consisted of men and women who either worked for architects or were architects and would work for me at night. There was no such thing as an eight-hour day. There was no difference between daylight and dark. I was on the make; I was after the jobs; I was getting the jobs constructed. I could always get good men because I would pay more money than anybody else.

By 1927 I had an organization, and I had developed a chain of command. The organization was divided into two parts. The design, drafting, and bookkeeping departments, reception room, and my office were located on the sixth floor of the California Bank Building in Beverly Hills. The other section involved construction. I had bought a lot in the industrial district of Hollywood. On this lot we constructed a galvanized iron building about the size of a six-car garage to house the tools and equipment. The yard itself was used for storing pipe, cement, sand, topsoil, the sides and bottoms of the very large boxes that we used for boxing trees, and all the other paraphernalia now used by a professional landscape contractor. But landscape contractors didn't exist in that day. As the landscape architect, I had to do it all.

In December 1927, when I went to Europe for six weeks, the construction work on the various jobs went on just as if I had been in Los Angeles because I had finally put together a smoothly run organization. I had a business office; I had a good bookkeeper and receptionist; I had good draftsmen; I had a good head draftsman.

On the outside, I had an excellent superintendent—Clifford Crabtree, who was to stay with me for the next ten years. His background was that of a superintendent of construction of large buildings. He could build any kind of a building up to six stories in height. He was a good diplomat, knew how to get along with the various county and city governments, knew how and where to obtain the necessary permits. He was excellent at his job; he was my shadow and took all that type of work off my shoulders.

I had a man, Dick Anderson, who did nothing but buy very large shrubs already in the ground. He not only bought the shrubs, but I had trained him so that he knew exactly how to get them out of the ground and box them. We had a connection with a very reliable trucking concern, and they could truck anything for us.

I had a man, Wayne Burger, who kept an index of all available plant materials. He not only knew the names of the various plants, but he knew how to spell and pronounce them—that was more than I could do. Wayne Burger's job was to keep track of all the plant materials the various nurseries had, so that no matter what we needed on a job, he knew where to get it.

I had draftsmen to make the working drawings; I had people to construct the gardens; I had an organization—things were swimming. Then I employed a young woman, Miss Johnson, who knew all about plants. She knew how to combine plants for foliage effect. She knew where plants would grow. No longer would I have to sit up at night making a plant list, trying to spell the names. She could do that. I directed that the plants should be foolproof—that is, tolerant of unfavorable soils, poor water, and a dry climate; that they would not need much attention. Miss Johnson was a find—she was great. I had one less worry; one less thing for me to do. More time to get more clients—more time to supervise the jobs—more time to keep the clients happy.

I, of course, was the salesman. I was the public relations man. No one talked to the clients but me. Everything was handled through me. In this way there was no confusion, and the organization worked. We had a smoothly run organization, and everyone knew where he or she fit into it.

European Trip, 1927

By November 1927 I had completed all of the preliminary work on the Harold Lloyd estate. Sumner Spaulding, the architect on the project, was going full blast. Unfortunately, I could do no further landscaping until the house was brought to completion. Since I had

some unexpected free time, I decided that my wife and I would take our honeymoon, even if it was seven years late. We would go to Europe. We'd see the Villa Gamberaia and all the other things that Spaulding had been talking about.

This European trip was to be a revelation to me as a landscape architect. Although I had seen impressive gardens after World War I, in Paris and England, I had yet to experience the marvels of the gardens and buildings in southern Europe—sights that were to strongly influence my future gardens in Southern California.

Our first important stop was Rome. In a few beauty-filled days we saw most of Rome. We had maps; we had a Baedeker; we had a Michelin Guide; we saw everything; we were overwhelmed. We went to the Spanish Steps, where they sell flowers. We walked up these steps to the French Academy at the top. We saw the

Villa Medici, Rome, Italy (photograph: A. E. Hanson, 1931).

Villa Medici—that lovely Palladian-type building. We looked across from the Villa Medici over to St. Peter's and saw the famous fountain in front of the villa. That was the same fountain we would copy for the Harold Lloyd estate the next year. We went out to Frascati; went out to the Villa d'Este. All the sights of Rome were marvels to us.

On to Florence and more beautiful sights—Michelangelo's incomparable David, the Duomo, the Pitti Palace, the Boboli gardens behind the palace. We made a special point of visiting the Villa Gamberaia, which Sumner Spaulding had praised so highly. Despite its rundown condition, I could understand why Spaulding was so impressed with this lovely Tuscan villa. My familiarity with it was to stand me in good stead in future work for Harold Lloyd.

Heading south to Spain for more memorable experiences, we went to Granada—Washington Irving's Granada. We saw the Alhambra,

and the world changed for me. We went to the Generalife—every landscape architect should go there. It defies the imagination. The gardens of the Alhambra at Granada and of that Moorish, Andalusian part of Spain—these are the kind of gardens we should have in Southern California—not Southern California in its entirety, but in Los Angeles. Southern California has many climates, but Los Angeles has a climate very near to that of Andalusia and Moorish Spain. This is true of Palm Springs as well.

Cordova was lovely. It was everything you could want or expect—one small court after another, at a widening in the street or where two streets come together. Each court in the very narrow streets had a little fountain in it, not just an ordinary fountain. They all had small pools with spouts, and were tiled with Spanish colored tiles—yellow and blue. Pots of flowers were everywhere. Nothing can surpass these potted

flowers in Cordova. This impression, too, was filed away in my mental notes for future gardens at home.

Cordova also has a city ordinance that every house in the city must be painted once a year. And every house has to have a dado, a band about two feet wide painted around the bottom of the building, so that when the dado becomes splashed from the muddy, cobblestoned streets, you merely repaint the dado, not the entire building. Cordova's houses are all alike—white with a tile roof and blue dado—the effect is irresistible.

We went on to Ronda and saw the famous garden by Forestier. Of course it was a very modern garden, but it was inspired by the old Moorish gardens. It had a channel of water going down the middle of each path. Everywhere in Moorish Spain these channels are used in the gardens. They are only about two inches wide and deep, and the water runs down them. This refreshes the atmo-

Left: Villa Cicogna, Bisuschio, Italy (photograph: A. E. Hanson, 1931).

Right: Villa Falconieri, Frascati, Italy (photograph: A. E. Hanson, 1931).

sphere and gives some humidity to a very dry climate. This concept was to prove useful to me later in gardens at home.

Next we visited Seville, beautiful Seville. We saw the tower where Spain had stored all the gold she had taken out of the Americas. The incomparable Maria Luisa Park was all that I had been dreaming about—rooms of gardens formed by plants and walls. You never saw more than one of them at a time. You turned to your left or right and came to another garden or room. There were large date-palm trees overhead, creating flickering shadows, spots of sunlight and shadow. Channels of water ran down the middle of the paths into low pools—actually basins of water in all conceivable shapes, not over ten inches deep, all tiled with glazed ceramic tiles in yellows and blues. These truly exceptional gardens had everything—tile benches, white pigeons, pots, and more pots, pools—small pools, large pools with spouts of water—thin jets of water coming from the nozzle—some nozzles made of ceramic, some of metal.

My head was bursting with ideas of garden designs in Seville. As you walked down the narrow streets and looked in through the front grill gate, you saw a patio or a little court. Every court had a small, shallow pool with a nozzle and a splash of water. Any one of these pools could be put to good use in Los Angeles.

After a rather hurried exposure to the exotic Moorish traditions of Tangier and the beauties of Portugal, we decided it was time to move north, to the beautiful gardens of Paris and Versailles.

I was particularly interested in seeing the gardens of Versailles because the previous year I had read a book, *The Smaller Houses and Gardens of Versailles from 1680 to 1815,* by Leigh French, Jr. and Harold Donaldson Eberlein (1920). The book pointed out that some of the nobility who had to live at the court of Louis XIV built small, compact townhouses in the city of Versailles to escape the pomp and ceremony of the court and to have some family life. These establishments were completely walled in, and the outside world was shut out.

When I visited Versailles in the winter of 1927, I took *Smaller Houses and Gardens of Versailles* with me. The book included the street addresses of the houses, and we drove around in a taxi looking at the exteriors. It was impossible to get permission to enter the gardens, but a number of these houses were located on corners. That allowed us to drive on the side streets where the taxi could pull up next to the wall so that I could get on the roof of the taxi to see the gardens.

One garden, fortunately on a corner, was No. 93 Rue Royale. The garden was lovely, and I could see most of it from the roof of the taxicab. While I was looking at these small, walled-in gardens, I thought, "Wouldn't it be lovely to do that sort of a landscape job in the heart of Los Angeles?" I made up my mind to do one of those gardens when the right client came along.

After Paris and Versailles we flew to England. Through the kindness of Harold Lloyd, I had letters of introduction to see some English gardens. My only problem with these landed British aristocrats was trying to satisfy their insatiable

Villa d'Este, Cernobbio, Italy (photograph: A. E. Hanson, 1931).

Villa Sergardi, Siena, Italy (photograph: A. E. Hanson, 1931).

curiosity about the Hollywood life—about Chaplin, Pickford, Fairbanks, and most of all, Harold Lloyd. Fielding all their Hollywood questions was costing me valuable garden-visiting time, so I finally stopped telling them what I did and for whom I worked.

England was fascinating—flowers everywhere and one green lawn after another. Unfortunately, of course, none of it would apply to what we were doing in Los Angeles. What would apply in Los Angeles were the Alhambra, the Generalife, and Maria Luisa Park, brick walks with channels of water down the middle, little inner courts. These were some of the ideas my European trip gave me. I couldn't wait to get home and try them out in Los Angeles. And my trip was worthwhile. I was soon to get clients for whom I would create gardens using these ideas—the Lockharts, the Youngs, the Cochrans, and, in 1932, the Dan Murphys. And that's the real story of *An Arcadian Landscape.*

October 29, 1929

I was at my project on the Kirk B. Johnson garden, getting ready to give the superintendent the weekly payroll checks, when Mr. Johnson came out, greatly agitated, and said, "Stop all work! Fire everybody! The stock market has crashed! We're all broke! The country's going to be bankrupt!"

We did stop all work on the Johnson garden. We didn't build the little pools in the north garden. We didn't build the lovely hillside garden that we had designed. Looking back, it was probably a blessing in disguise, because the maintenance costs would have been very high.

I was greatly disturbed by Mr. Johnson's attitude and contacted my banker. He said, "Don't worry, Hanson. It'll work out. You'll get your money." And, in the end, I did.

But the world had changed. A life style had come to an end. It

had changed, just as much as the life style in France when Marie Antoinette went to the guillotine.

Black Thursday brought many changes to landscape architecture.

I had designed a garden for a wholesale jeweler in New Windsor Square (That's the area north of Third) before the crash. I won't give you his real name—I'll call him Mr. Goldstein. I did the Goldstein garden in 1928 and spent about $15,000 on the back yard. It was an attractive formal garden. I still think it was good. He paid the bills promptly, and the family enjoyed their garden living.

In 1931 I got a call from Mr. Goldstein. He said, "Hanson, do you remember me?"

I said, "Sure, Mr. Goldstein, very pleasant memories."

"Well," he said, "you know it's a different kind of a world today, and our life style has changed. I've bought a small home."

He gave me the address, a very modest neighborhood. He said, "I

Left: Alhambra, Granada, Spain (photograph: A. E. Hanson, 1931).

Right: Casa de Rey, Ronda, Spain (photograph: A. E. Hanson, 1931).

12

wonder if you'd mind coming over and giving me a little advice. I'd certainly appreciate it. I haven't any money to spend, but we always enjoyed the Windsor Square garden.''

I said, ''Of course. I'll be over at nine o'clock tomorrow morning.''

I no longer had a landscape architect's office, or a draftsman, or an organization for doing landscaping. I went over to see him the next morning. I gave him some suggestions and made a rough drawing on a piece of paper; he was delighted. He offered to pay me for the advice, but I wouldn't take the money.

I said, ''Yes, times have changed, but tell me something—which even today I can't understand. How could you people in 1928 have been so nonchalant about how you spent your money?''

''Well,'' he said, ''what was money? I would play golf in the mornings three times a week back in 1928, with a certain group, of which Sid Grauman was one. [Sid Grauman was the originator of the plush million-dollar theaters.] We'd play the first nine holes [all golf courses were laid out so that after you played nine holes, you were back at the clubhouse to start the next nine], and before teeing off at the tenth hole, our foursome would go in and look at the bulletin board to see what the stock market had done. And hell, it was nothing to have made $10,000 while we played the first nine holes. So, why shouldn't I spend it? I could always make more.''

They were certainly affluent years.

I did a garden in 1929 for ''Mr. Ben Square.'' He had the musical-instrument concession in a large department store—pianos, radios, phonographs—and was also the owner of a chain of music stores. He had a nice house in the Griffith Park area. He wanted to

build a tennis court and redo the landscaping.

There was no possible place to put the tennis court, because the property was all hillside. But he wanted it, so we built it—just as you would build an office building on the side of a hill. We used a reinforced concrete structure, with a concrete slab on the top. Money was no object.

For the two-week period ending October 1929, the bill owed to me for money advanced for the job was several thousand dollars, which I had already paid out of my own pocket. ''Mr. Square'' called me on the telephone, greatly agitated, two days after the stock-market crash, and said, ''Hanson, come down to the store at once. It's very important.'' He said, ''Hanson, I'm broke. I can't pay you a nickel. It's only a matter of days before the sheriff walks in here. Look around the store and see what you want. Pick it out. Never mind what it costs.''

I picked out a Chickering baby grand piano, rosewood finish, Ampico player; that was the only instrument Mrs. Hanson or I could play. Six months later, I sold it for $350 cash. By that time, the family had to have the money to buy food.

''Mr. Ben Square'' was a square-shooter. He didn't have to warn me. So, that's another reason to call the 1920s the incredible years.

20/20 Hindsight

When we returned from our European trip, we were still living on Almont Drive. Too bad we didn't stay there, but we got infected with that ''money bug''—money coming unbelievably easily. So, like the rest of the fools, we bought an expensive two-story house on Linden Drive in Beverly Hills.

The house was set back about sixty feet, built in sort of an ''L,'' so that I could put in a high wall on a line with the front of the house to create a front patio. I built a little bit of a garden in that patio, with one of those small, tiled pools I'd seen in the Maria Luisa Park—with three spouts of water in it. The pool, made of glazed tile, was about six inches deep. I moved three large pepper trees to the front of the house between the high wall and the curb, put in a wide tile path across the front and many pots.

In the rear I created a little formal garden such as those I had seen in the Generalife. I put in it a pool with scalloped edges like the pool you see when you first enter the Generalife. I went to an expert cast-stone maker in Pasadena to have the pool made. I had twelve of those pools made and eventually put the remaining eleven in various gardens.

The twenties were unbelievable. Everybody had money; everybody spent money, just as though it were water. It was too bad someone wasn't around to remind us of what the world was really like; to remind us that we were just the bubbles on the top of the champagne; to remind us of the Midnight Mission on Main Street—and the poor bums, the drunks, the alcoholics, the people sleeping in alleys, the people who didn't have enough to eat; to remind us that we were in a mad, mad world.

But we certainly had a lot of fun. There was Bill Menzies, who later became the art director for *Gone with the Wind;* there was a casting director for Fox; there was a stock broker. We'd all sit around at our house with bootleg liquor, fried chicken, and one man playing the piano while we sang, drank, and ate chicken. Time meant nothing on a Sunday night. We'd sing ribald songs like ''Lydia Pinkham'' and improvise new rhymes. It was fun. We were going to reap the harvest, but we didn't know it. Maybe it was just as well.

Here I was, a landscape architect—a non-college man—and I was making all kinds of money. It came easily. I had all kinds of work. I had all kinds of satisfied clients. I could do anything I wanted. We had domestic help; we had a nurse; we had expenses, expenses, and more expenses. The time was going to come when I wished we were still living on Almont Drive without those expenses. We had four youngsters by then.

In the spring of 1928, I was going full blast on Harold Lloyd's estate; I was able to finish that job. Many things happened that were fortunate.

From February 1928 to October 29, 1929, was an unforgettable time—an incredible time! It's hard to believe it. During that period I constructed many, many gardens, costing thousands and tens of thousands of dollars. It got to the point that I wouldn't bother with any garden that didn't cost $10,000 or more. Lee Rombotis, my designer, could carry out my ideas. He could make drawings,

sketches, and renderings; he had imagination. I could point my finger, and he could do it.

In that brief time I did the gardens that this book is really about: the Harold Lloyd estate, the Kirk B. Johnson garden, the George I. Cochran garden, the Lockhart garden, the Archibald Young garden. They were all different. Yet they were all the same in a way—they cost money, money, money. What was money? Everybody had money—that is, all the people that interested a landscape architect had money.

Looking back, I still think those gardens were good. And then October 29, 1929, the stock market crashed. We woke up with an awful headache. It was the morning after, and we were going to have a hangover.

But even if October 29, 1929, hadn't come along, I would no longer have continued in the profession of landscape architecture, specializing in private residential gardens. I had an itch. I wanted to create communities and develop small villages. I wanted to apply to a piece of land everything I had learned from 1912 to 1929.

I wanted to own the land myself, and I wanted to be the boss. I wanted to carry out my own ideas without consulting anyone. I thought I could get all the money I wanted. I had wealthy clients who believed in me, who wanted to make investments. I made up my mind that I would be a land developer. This was before the twenty-ninth of October, 1929.

Eventually I did become a land developer. I was always lucky. In February 1930, with the stock market crashing, along came Frank Vanderlip, the retired New York financier and banker. He was the owner of 12,000 acres of the Rancho Los Palos Verdes, with ten miles of shoreline, and he wanted to see the Harold Lloyd gardens. The Lloyd Corporation asked me if I would be good enough to show him through the gardens. I was delighted.

Another world opened for me. I was to become a land developer. I was to become executive vice president of the Palos Verdes Corporation. And I was to do communities; first Rolling Hills and then Hidden Hills—and those are two later stories.

The Harry Calendar Garden Windsor Square

1922

Harry Calendar had made his money the hard, slow way as an insurance broker. He had invested some money in the drilling of an oil well in the Los Angeles basin. It came in. He reinvested the profits in more oil wells and became quite wealthy.

His home was in Windsor Square, the second block north of Wilshire Boulevard. It was a typical rectangular city lot, about 80 x 190 feet, in a well-established, good residential area, conveniently close to the business section of Los Angeles.

The house was on the east side of the street, which was ideal from the standpoint of garden living because the rear garden and existing porch were protected from the prevailing afternoon breeze. One could sit on the porch in the afternoon with the light at one's back so that the shadows and the light in the garden would be soft.

The Calendar house was three years old. It was square, stucco, two-story with a red tile roof, and of a pleasing off-white color. The driveway on the north side led straight back to a two-story garage on the northeast corner.

The property had well-cared-for front and back lawns and some shrubs at the base of the house. The garden was planted with miscellaneous shrubbery at both sides and in the back.

Mr. Calendar liked what I suggested for his garden. I built a generous-sized terrace at the back of the house, floored with dark red tile and roofed with an attractive awning. At the end of the porch, I built a small pool, two feet in diameter, eighteen inches deep, with a yellow and blue tile rim. I bought a small gargoyle for the center—a little bit of a figure, twelve inches high, that would spout water—and the overflow would feed a small stream. At the end of the porch we had a sunken grass panel. On the right-hand side of the panel, the stream meandered down to a small, naturalistic lily pool.

At the rear of the garden I erected a small colonial-style pergola of the type that you could buy from any good lumber yard. At the back of the pergola, in the center, I built a curved niche made of plaster and chicken wire, containing a small, draped female statue playing the pipes.

Calendar Garden, Windsor Square, Los Angeles, 1922. View of the garden from the living room. The garden itself begins with a small pool and terminates with a pergola.

On the left I put in a heavy screening of shrubbery that blocked the view of the garage. I flood-lighted the garden by erecting a nail keg that resembled a birdhouse on the top of a four-by-four (nails came in wooden kegs in those days). The light was inside of the keg, on the side away from the house, and situated so that it would floodlight the lily pool. The top of the birdhouse had a small weather-vane of a sunflower and two ducks.

None of this was expensive, but it was landscape architecture. I did the garden, not as a horticulturist, but as a professional landscape architect.

Calendar Garden, Windsor Square, Los Angeles, 1922. The pool at the start of the garden.

Calendar Garden, Windsor Square, Los Angeles, 1922. The terminal of the garden.

Calendar Garden, Windsor Square, Los Angeles, 1922. A birdhouse made from a wooden nail keg used to floodlight the garden.

Calendar Garden, Windsor Square, Los Angeles, 1922. A naturalistic lily pool, hidden to the side of the garden.

The Harry Calendar Garden
Bel Air
1923

Mr. Calendar called me one morning and said, "Archie, I want you to go out with me to Bel Air because I've got my eye on a couple of acres of land. I'd just like to have a place where I can get away by myself. It's kind of out in the country, not too far from town, and I could just sit around and forget about everything. I don't want to build a house on it. I want you to go out there with me and see what you can do with it."

It was a beautiful one-and-one-half-acre piece of hillside situated across the road from the number-four hole of the Bel Air Golf Course. It wasn't going to be very many years before this little piece of wild country would be surrounded by expensive homes.

I built an entranceway, set back about twelve feet from the road, out of Santa Susana sandstone and constructed a heavy plank redwood door. I burnt the redwood with a blowtorch and scrubbed it out with a wire brush to bring out the grain, then soaked it heavily with linseed oil, and used a copy of an old Spanish knocker for the handle.

A little way up the hill I built a picnic area with a flagstone floor, an outdoor grill, and a spit. We also built a counter with a sink and some cupboards.

A little farther up we built a small building, again out of Santa Susana rubble, with a red tile roof.

The building had plumbing facilities and a small room where Mr. Calendar could take a nap. It also had a toolroom.

One day when Mr. Calendar and I were prowling around the hill, I came to a spot and I said, "Mr. Calendar, you know we could have a waterfall here. It would be interesting."

And he said, "All right, let's do it."

So we did. We helped nature out a bit to make the waterfall, by doing a little cutting back into the bank. We built a path about six feet in front of the waterfall where we put a redwood bridge with an iron railing crossing the stream. The view from that bridge was lovely. You could sit on the covered seat near the bridge, look across the golf course, and see the ocean in the distance.

I was up there in the early part of 1977, fifty-four years after I built that rustic seat and the bridge and, unbelievably, they are still there. Redwood is pretty good stuff.

Calendar Garden, Bel Air, 1923. The entranceway, constructed of Santa Susana sandstone.

The waterfall went down to a pool stocked with goldfish and lilies. An electric pump recycled the water. Mr. Calendar was very fond of the outdoors. He had been in the redwoods north of San Francisco and enjoyed the trillium and other native plants he saw there. He thought maybe he could have those plants on his place in Bel Air. So I got in touch with Mr. Carl Purdy of Ukiah, who was a specialist in Northern California native plants. We tried Lady Slippers, trillium, and other Northern California plants. Unfortunately, they did not do well. After all, we had a semidesert climate. Mr. Calendar didn't mind spending the money. He enjoyed every minute of the making of the garden.

Mr. Calendar called the property The Oaks, joshed with me about some of his acquaintances' referring to it as his estate, and he said, "Archie, a couple of acres isn't an estate; maybe a hundred is." That shows you what kind of a man he was. He loved nature and was not a bit pretentious—did not put on airs.

Later, the Calendar Bel Air gardens were donated to UCLA; they are now known as the Japanese gardens, and the entrance is of Japanese architecture.

Calendar Garden, Bel Air, 1923. The waterfall, ten feet high. In the upper part of this picture is the bridge. This photograph was taken fifty-seven years after the completion of the garden.

The Harold Lloyd Garden
Beverly Hills
1925-29

Harold Lloyd and A.E.H.

In the spring of 1925, I received a phone call from Mrs. Sam Taylor. I had made a garden for Mr. and Mrs. Taylor the year before. Mr. Taylor had been Harold Lloyd's director for many years. Mrs. Taylor told me that her husband had made an appointment for me with Harold Lloyd for the next afternoon.

I was at Harold Lloyd's office not at two o'clock, the appointed time, but at 1:45 and was ushered into his office promptly at two o'clock. I had never before seen Harold Lloyd except in his movies and, of course, he was then in make-up. In person he was not at all as I had imagined. He looked like a successful business executive. After telling me that Mr. Taylor had highly recommended me, Harold Lloyd said that he had just purchased eleven acres in Beverly Hills, where he wanted to have a fine home. He and his wife had one child, a one-year-old girl. He was the personification of warmth and charm. I was his exact age, almost to the month. I spent about half an hour with him, and we made an appointment to meet the next afternoon on the property.

The next day at three o'clock, I was waiting at the property. Up drove a beautiful, tan Rolls-Royce touring car. It was the most beautiful auto I had ever seen. And, in the years since, I've never seen an automobile that has given me the thrill that *that* one did! Harold Lloyd sat in the front seat beside his uniformed chauffeur—a big, burly, good-natured-looking man of about fifty. The glamour of Harold Lloyd, Douglas Fairbanks, Charlie Chaplin, and Mary Pickford was so great, it was necessary for movie stars to be protected from being mobbed by their fans.

Harold Lloyd got out of his car, shook hands with me, and took me to the southern corner of his property on Benedict Canyon Road. We started to walk along the Benedict Canyon frontage to the northern corner—1,400 feet. Having an outdoor profession, I was used to tramping over land. I was thin and wiry and in good physical shape. But at the end of the 1,400 feet, I was out of breath keeping up with Harold Lloyd. For him it was a breeze! Movies in those days were really movies. The action moved. All of Harold Lloyd's films

Harold Lloyd Garden, Beverly Hills, 1925–29. Aerial photo, taken in the 1930s, from above the tennis court, looking toward the Beverly Hills Hotel.

involved a chase—the good guys after the bad guys, or the other way around. For that reason, he had to keep himself in top physical condition. Although he played the part of a young man about to enter college—say about eighteen years old—he was actually thirty-two. He had to train just as hard as any prize fighter to keep his weight down.

We turned around and walked back toward the southern end of the land, where there was an old wagon road. We took it up to the top of the hill, where he said he wanted to locate his home. After we had walked back down, he turned to me and said, waving his arms, "Do you suppose I could have a golf course here?" "Here" was a land bordered by Benedict Canyon Road and the toe of the hill. Through the middle of this

land ran a dry wash with a meandering channel. Everything was overgrown by weeds and shrubs. I was stunned. It looked impossible. But nothing seemed beyond me that day, and I blithely said, "I don't see why not! I'll think it over and call you tomorrow."

He left and I again walked the 1,400 feet and looked at the toe of the slope and the dry wash. I estimated that the size of this bottom land was about four acres—and on that God-forsaken piece of land, I had said I thought we could put in a golf course. I got in my car and drove on the wagon road to where it crossed the dry wash and stopped. I sat with my head in my hands and thought how foolish I had been even to think about the possibility of a golf course. But the die was cast.

The Bel Air Golf Course had been built several years earlier by the Alphonso Bell Corporation. Alphonso Bell had been an orange rancher in Sante Fe Springs. He was very astute. He believed that underlying his land was an oil pool, and he quietly acquired options on the surrounding acreage. Then he went to an oil company and got them to drill a well. It came in—and it was a gusher! It drowned his orange grove in oil. He was an instant millionaire.

But he was not content just to sit still. He had been a tennis champion, and his doubles partner had been Claude Wayne, vice president of a local life insurance company. Mr. Bell and Mr. Wayne formed the Alphonso Bell Corporation. They purchased 26,000 acres just west of Beverly

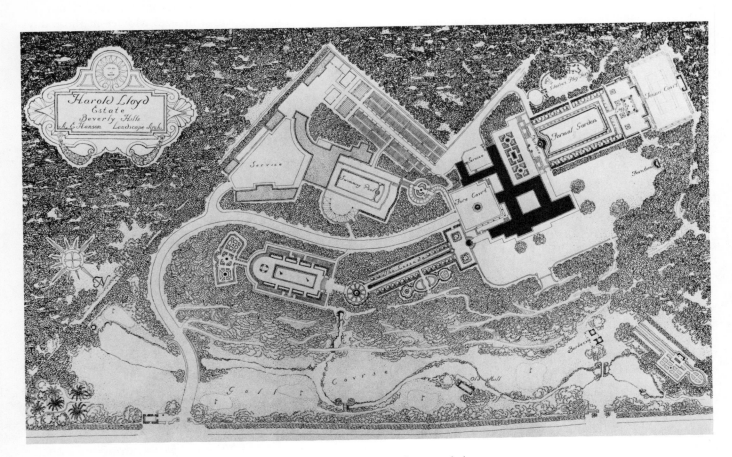

Harold Lloyd Garden, Beverly Hills, 1925–29. The plot plan made after completion.

Hills, created the Bel Air community, and developed the Bel Air Golf Course.

Claude Wayne was an old and close friend. The minute I got to my office, I phoned Claude and said I had just left Harold Lloyd (All the world knew who Harold Lloyd was!), who had eleven acres in the heart of Beverly Hills. If I could think of a way to develop a small golf course of some kind, I could get the landscape job—and I would be made, professionally. And who was the golf architect for

Harold Lloyd Garden, Beverly Hills, 1925–29. An aerial photograph of Benedict Canyon Road adjacent to the Harold Lloyd estate.

Harold Lloyd Garden, Beverly Hills, 1925–29. A view taken when we first started to grade the upper ten acres. The trees are on the neighbor's property. The skyline is Santa Monica Bay and Malibu. The hilltop had been eroded; there was no topsoil.

Harold Lloyd Garden, Beverly Hills, 1925–29. Commencing to grade for the house site. Two teams of animals are shown grading. The cypresses in the upper left-hand corner were dead and were removed.

Harold Lloyd Garden, Beverly Hills, 1925–29. An aerial photograph taken November 29, 1926, shows the golf course completed, and the curved bridge. The lower end of the library garden—the "Villa d'Este" lily pool with the suntrap—has been completed. The pergola of the cutting garden, lath houses, and glass houses are also finished. In the upper middle, on the left-hand side of the photograph, is the completed tennis court with its spectators' shelter. The formal garden pavilion has been started.

the Bel Air Golf Course? Claude said the course was designed by George Thomas, who had designed many of the finest golf courses in America. But he was an extremely wealthy man and didn't do it for money, only as a hobby, so I couldn't possibly hire him. Thomas did have an associate, Billy Bell, who did all the engineering, completed all of Thomas's plans, and constructed the courses. Bell was a professional; he did it for money.

I immediately phoned Billy Bell, telling him of the situation, and how advantageous the Harold Lloyd connection could be to him and to me. If I got the landscaping, he would do the golf course. And due to Harold Lloyd's prominence, we would be "some pun'kins." I was enough of a salesman to convince Bill Bell to meet me on the property the next morning. We spent an hour

Harold Lloyd Garden, Beverly Hills, 1925–29. In March 1925 Harold Lloyd said, waving his arms as he stood in the middle of this dry wash, "Do you suppose I could have a golf course here?"

Harold Lloyd Garden, Beverly Hills, 1925–29. And here at the exact spot, in the summer of 1926, is the former dry wash, now the water hazard for his golf course.

22

Harold Lloyd Garden, Beverly Hills, 1925–29. The southerly view of the driveway bridge over the canoe course. It was of reinforced concrete, with a veneer of adobe-colored Santa Susana sandstone. The keystone is an elaborately carved decoration.

Harold Lloyd Garden, Beverly Hills, 1925–29. The dovecote at lake #3, built almost on the property line. To the right of the structure is the southernmost green. The dovecote housed the equipment for raising and lowering the gate used to control storm water.

Harold Lloyd Garden, Beverly Hills, 1925–29. The golf course. This course was built for pros and expert amateurs.

Harold Lloyd Garden, Beverly Hills, 1925–29. The mill in the lower garden. One of my favorite photographs of the gardens I created.

and a half there, and the upshot was that he took an old envelope out of his pocket and sketched out five greens and five tees. He said, "You know, I think we could work it so that a golfer could play twenty-seven holes without repeating the same route." (This could be done by doubling back to certain of the greens.) He said it wouldn't be a toy course; it would be a fine test of golf, and the best of the pros and amateurs would enjoy playing it. I was very encouraged.

At noon I phoned Harold Lloyd at the studio, and he again met me late in the afternoon on the property. We walked around and I waved my arms and told him about Billy Bell. I showed him the old envelope with the location of the five greens and five tees.

I said, "Mr. Lloyd, who is your architect?"

And he said, "I haven't got an architect."

And I said to myself, "I'm going to get the Harold Lloyd landscaping job, and I'm going to get the architect for Mr. Lloyd, and the architect is going to be under obligation to me, instead of the other way around."

I thought to myself, "I'll introduce four architects to Mr. Lloyd, and they will all be architects that I have done work for, or men I know I can get along with—because doing a large estate is going to take a lot of teamwork between the landscape architect and the architect."

As Harold Lloyd was getting into his car, he asked, "When will I hear from you?"

Harold Lloyd Garden, Beverly Hills, 1925–29. The completed old mill, with the waterwheel in operation. The water that was not used for turning the waterwheel created a small waterfall.

I said, "Well, I want some time to think it over and dream about it. I'll get in touch with you in a few days."

This was March 1925. At daylight the next morning I arrived at the property. I walked, and walked over most of the property. I couldn't walk the hillside. It was too steep. Some of it was almost straight up and down, and all of it was covered with poison oak and nettles.

I went up to the top of the hill, where Harold Lloyd said he wanted to have his home. The trouble was, he owned only half of the hill. If he owned all of the hill, he could place his home on the top and enjoy a 360-degree view. He would have a perfect homesite. I figured he would have to acquire about five more acres.

I thought constantly about Harold Lloyd's estate and how to landscape it. It was useless for me to think about the upper ten acres (I was already assuming he would buy the additional five acres), because that landscaping would depend upon the kind of home to be built. But the four acres along Benedict Canyon Road could be developed independently of the rest of the land, as could the two acres of the steep hillside. I had all kinds of schemes in my head for the four acres, and I worked them around and around until I wore them out. But the landscaping of that four acres was starting to jell.

All day Sunday, four days after I had first met Harold Lloyd, I sprawled on my living-room floor, which was littered with landscape books and pictures. I stopped for lunch and went back to work—and I stewed. And then I knew what I wanted to do. I closed the landscape books and put them back in the bookcase.

On Monday morning I phoned Harold Lloyd and made an appointment to see him that afternoon at his office. At three o'clock I spread out on his office floor a large contour map of his property, without a pencil mark on it. I began to tell him about the golf course. Harold Lloyd had been intrigued that first day when I said I thought he could have a golf course.

I put my finger on the map at the northeast corner of his property on Benedict Canyon Road and starting there, traced the dry wash as it paralleled, more or less, Benedict Canyon Road down to the southern boundary line of his property. I showed him how Billy Bell had placed two greens on the western side of the dry wash and three greens on the eastern side.

Then again, I put my finger on the map at the northeast corner of his property and drew an outline of a small lake, then a little stream, and then another lake. And I said that where this stream connected the two lakes, we would have a small stone bridge, like the bridges in the Northern English countryside.

I said here we would have a picnic ground and a barbecue pit that would take a side of beef. We would have an outdoor grill; we would have an old-fashioned spit for roasting a turkey. At the end of our second lake, we would let the water flow down a creek, fifty feet. At this point there was an abrupt change of grade, of about six feet. Here we would have an old mill, with a waterwheel, and that could be our golf clubhouse. Starting at the old mill—and this really surprised him—we'd start a canoe course, and he could paddle a canoe for 800 feet in the heart of Beverly Hills. The canoe course would also be a water hazard for the golf course.

I would create the canoe course by building a dam at the extreme southern end of the dry wash, and at this point we would have another lake. We would have a golf course and a canoe course, but what it was really all going to look like was a bit of countryside—real countryside, like Northern England and Southern Scotland. Who had

Harold Lloyd Garden, Beverly Hills, 1925–29. Harold Lloyd (wearing the cap) and six pros, some of the finest in the world. In the distance, on the right, are some members of the press.

25

ever heard of doing all of this in the heart of Beverly Hills?

I glanced at him from the corner of my eye, and I could see that I was doing all right. Then I went on to tell him of all the ways I wanted to create that countryside. My finger was becoming shorter and shorter, because I was still using it as a pointer. I stopped for breath.

Harold Lloyd said, "*You're* my Landscape Architect!" (I almost fainted.) "And what is your first name?"

"Well," I said, "it's Arch. That stands for Archibald."

He said, "What's your middle initial?"

I said it was "E," and he said, "What's that stand for?"

It was bad enough to tell him my first name was Archibald (because in 1925 Archibald was a sissy name given to comic characters), but then I said, "The 'E' stands for Elexis. And isn't that a hell of a thing to have for a name?"

I guess emotionally, I was on edge. I was going to be *the Landscape Architect of the Los Angeles area.*

Harold Lloyd Garden, Beverly Hills, 1925–29. The rear of the barbecue house. On the left is the barbecue pit, with its chimney.

He said, "Oh, no! I'm going to call you A. E., and *you're my landscape architect,* and you call me Harold."

I said, "No, Mr. Lloyd. You call me A. E.—that's fine—that's the best nickname I could have. But as long as you're paying me as your landscape architect, you're Mr. Lloyd. And any of my employees who calls you Harold is fired. When I get my last paycheck, you're Harold—but not before."

"Okay, A. E., if you want it that way. When do we go to work?"

I said, "Tomorrow."

Harold Lloyd Garden, Beverly Hills, 1925–29. This is the cooking section of the barbecue building. The grill is on the left, bake oven underneath, copper utensils on the wall.

Harold Lloyd Garden, Beverly Hills, 1925–29. Harold Lloyd, Charles Chaplin, Douglas Fairbanks—the three kings of the movies—leaning against one side of the barbecue building. It has been stated that Harold Lloyd made more money than the other two put together.

He said, "That's fine. But I'm really a corporation, although I'm the sole stockholder. I have a board of directors. They handle all of the money details. My uncle Bill Frazer is the general manager of the Harold Lloyd Corporation, and he and the rest of the directors will want some kind of an ironclad understanding—a written contract. You and I don't need anything, but they need it. We've got to satisfy them."

I met the next morning with the board of directors, composed of five men. They drew up a business contract. I signed it and went to work.

After I had made satisfactory arrangements with the board of directors, I again saw Harold Lloyd. Using a map, I showed him why it was advisable for him to acquire the rest of the hill. He could see that the eleven acres contained only half of the top of the hill, and that by acquiring the additional five acres, he would have a perfect homesite and absolute privacy. Harold Lloyd was able to purchase the additional five acres the next week, so we then had sixteen acres—four acres along Benedict Canyon Road, two acres of steep hillside, and ten acres on top.

The landscaping of our fairyland golf course was not dependent on the architecture of the home to be built on the top of the hill. However, nothing could be done with the upper ten acres until we had an architect and the home had been designed.

Harold Lloyd did not have a specific architect nor any particular style of architecture in mind. He said that several architects had been recommended, but he had not talked to any of them. He asked if I had someone in mind. I had been giving the selection of the architect a great deal of thought and had determined that the first architect I would recommend would be Reginald Johnson, who

was considered the top residential architect in the western United States. I got in touch with Johnson, who was delighted that I had given his name to Harold Lloyd. He suggested that Harold Lloyd and I spend a day with him in Santa Barbara, because there were many fine estates in Montecito, Santa Barbara proper, and Hope Ranch. We could drive up, see three places in the morning, have lunch at El Paseo Restaurant, then see another three places at the Hope Ranch.

A few days later we went to Santa Barbara. We saw three homes before lunch—all of them stately and superb, owned and designed for mature people whose children had grown up and left home.

We had lunch at El Paseo Restaurant. After lunch we drove to Hope Ranch, where we were to see another three homes. We saw two of them, and then Harold Lloyd said, "I'm sorry, but I've got to get back to the lot [studio].

The boys will be wondering what has become of me."

That was a tip-off to me. I knew instantly that Harold Lloyd did not see eye-to-eye with Reginald Johnson. And I thought all the way back that it was up to me to see that I did not make the mistake again. I must get someone who would be compatible with Harold Lloyd. But who? I had three other architects in mind, but

Harold Lloyd Garden, Beverly Hills, 1925–29. A view of the underground storm drain, over which lakes #1 and #2 were built. The animals in this photograph are mules, pulling a small Fresno.

Harold Lloyd Garden, Beverly Hills, 1925–29. The stone bridge over the stream that connected lake #1 and lake #2. The picnic-barbecue building is to the left.

by the time we were halfway back to Hollywood, I had come to the conclusion that only one of the three would do, and that was *Sumner Spaulding.*

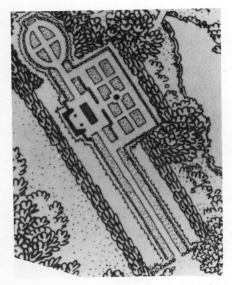

Harold Lloyd Garden, Beverly Hills, 1925–29. Plot plan of the north formal garden.

When we arrived at the studio, we got out of the car. Harold Lloyd said goodbye to Johnson and thanked him profusely. When Johnson left, Harold Lloyd said to me, "A. E., come in for a minute."

And the next remark, when we were inside his office, was, "Who else have you got on the list?"

When Harold Lloyd said, "Who's next?" I commented on what I knew his reaction had been to Johnson. And then I told him about Spaulding.

Harold Lloyd said, "Get him over here tomorrow if you can, and we'll see how the three of us get along."

Early the next morning I took Spaulding over the property and briefed him on our trip to Santa Barbara with Johnson.

In the afternoon Spaulding and I met with Harold Lloyd. Things went fine, and I knew that Harold Lloyd liked him.

Spaulding suggested that the three of us go back up to Santa Barbara as soon as convenient for Mr. Lloyd, because there were many fine estates in the area. Some of them had been built as far back as the 1880s. For years it had been the mecca for affluent people. There was always a yacht or two in the harbor, and two or three parlor cars parked at the railroad station. Spaulding commented that there were a number of different types of fine homes in the Santa Barbara area. There were Andalusian farm-houses, Spanish homes, various Italian and English homes, and so forth. A few hours devoted to driving around and looking at the ex-teriors might enable Harold Lloyd to find one particular style that he liked better than others.

We went to Santa Barbara in that beautiful Rolls-Royce and everything worked perfectly; the upshot was that in a week, Spaulding was the architect.

The Golf Course

Harold Lloyd was keenly interested in building the golf course. And we could begin building it at once. First we had to have a detailed contour map made of all the land from Benedict Canyon Road to the toe of the slope, starting at the southern corner on Benedict Canyon Road and going to the northern corner of the property on Benedict Canyon Road, a distance of 1,400 feet, and about four acres in size.

Meandering approximately through the middle of the width of this land was a dry wash, which, during the heavy rains, became a raging torrent as it drained all the water from several thousand acres to the north. One way the dry wash could be handled would be with an ordinary square concrete drain. The other method would be to make a canoe course of the

Harold Lloyd Garden, Beverly Hills, 1925–29. A view of the golf course from the "sample" formal garden we made on the course. Immediately to the right is the barbecue area. The bridge between lakes #1 and #2 is just barely distinguishable over the low wall, and beyond this bridge is the old mill.

wash's most southerly 800 feet and construct two lakes on the northerly balance of the land. This drainage work was complicated and had to be precisely engineered.

It took several months to grade the lower four acres, where the golf course would be developed. When that work was finished, I supplied Billy Bell with a contour map, and he finished his plans for the five greens and five tees. By the spring of 1926, Harold Lloyd was playing golf on his course.

When I met with Harold Lloyd that day in 1925, with a map spread out on his office floor, I had suggested a small golf clubhouse, and an old English mill with a waterwheel. So, when we had finished grading, I asked Joe Weston, an architect with whom I had worked, to look at something on the Harold Lloyd property.

Weston and his wife, on their honeymoon, had taken a walking trip around England and France, and he had an affinity for small

cottages and farm buildings— especially those made of stone.

I showed him the area at the end of the canoe course where I wanted to build our golf clubhouse. Joe thought it was great. In the next few days he showed me a number of sketches, and I picked

Harold Lloyd Garden, Beverly Hills, 1925–29. Harold Lloyd sitting on the well that was the start of the golf-course formal garden.

Harold Lloyd Garden, Beverly Hills, 1925–29. My theory of design was and is that every garden should have a starting point and a terminal. The well in the photograph right, above was the starting point of the small formal garden, and the small figurative sculpture at the end of the walk is the terminal.

Harold Lloyd Garden, Beverly Hills, 1925–29. Pan playing pipes is the terminal of our small formal garden. You would never dream that 50 feet away was busy Benedict Canyon Road.

Harold Lloyd Garden, Beverly Hills, 1925–29. The well at the end of the long walk.

out the one I liked the best. He then made a lovely little watercolor of it, which I showed to Harold Lloyd. He liked it, and we built it.

The exterior of the clubhouse was of that lovely, adobe-colored Santa Susana sandstone. The roof was of mission tile. Part of the building was two stories. The upper story was reached by an outside staircase and was used for a card room. The lower story contained the golf lockers. The floors were of cork tile to accommodate spiked golf shoes. The interior walls of both stories were finished with highly selected redwood, which had a beautiful grain and was of a lovely color, like old mahogany. We finished and polished it until it shone like the top of a grand piano.

The old mill, when it was finished, was highly satisfactory. It wasn't a fake—it was comfortable to look at—it fit into the landscape. It was Joe Weston's creation. The mill wheel really worked. It was quite a hassle to find out just exactly how to build it, and how much water to pour over it, but in the end everything worked out.

In 1926, during the Los Angeles Open Tournament, Harold Lloyd asked a number of the amateurs and pros to be his guests at his golf course. One of the pros, Joe Kirkwood, was known as a trickshot artist. He could make a golf ball go almost anywhere he wanted. He was also quite a prankster.

After a lunch of barbecued beef from Harold Lloyd's own barbecue pit, he and his guests walked over to the first tee opposite the old mill, and Joe Kirkwood said, "Doug [Douglas Fairbanks], let me have your pocket watch."

He took Fairbanks's watch, put it on the tee, nonchalantly put a golf ball on the crystal, took his driver, and drove the ball as hard as he could. Everyone gasped, thinking that Douglas Fairbanks's

watch would be in a thousand pieces, scattered all down the fairway. But there it was on the tee, and not a mark on it!

Harold Lloyd and his cronies enjoyed the golf course.

I think that an article published in *Better Homes and Gardens,* written by Elmer T. Peterson after an interview with Harold Lloyd, can give a better summary of the history of the golf course and what it was like, than I can. An excerpt from that article follows:
"I had three landscape architects give their opinion as to a golf course," he [Harold Lloyd] said. "Two of them said it couldn't be done and one said it could. So I accepted the minority report—and, well, there's the golf course."

There it was, sure enough, laid out in a narrow strip, perhaps not more than two or three acres in all, and it is pronounced good by no less authorities than Eddie Loos, George Von Elm, Harry Cooper, and Tommy Armour. Loos holds the course record with a 28. The course par is 32. It is not a miniature course, as might be suspected. There are two full wood shots and a number of mashies. "Every hole is a shot," said Lloyd. "No. 7 is the prize. It is about 100 yards, over the creek and beyond the big pepper trees. It takes a niblick and a push shot to get the ball on the green."

The Waterfall

I made it a practice to go to the Harold Lloyd job at least three times a week, spending an hour there. I would arrive at eight o'clock, when the crew started.

One April morning in 1926, I was checking on how well the golf greens were being maintained. When I arrived at green number 4, I happened to glance up to the top of the hill where the library

"Villa d'Este" lily pool was being constructed. I was surprised at how steep the hill was at that point and wondered if it would be practical to have a waterfall there.

I walked up to the lily pool and over to the edge of the bluff, looked down, and shrank back. It was like standing on the tenth floor of an office building without any wall in front of you, a sheer drop of 100 feet to the golf course.

I phoned the Harold Lloyd studio and asked if he could meet me at the estate. Harold Lloyd met me at the main gate, and we drove up to the lily pool. I took him to the edge of the bluff and had him look down. He instinctively shrank back. (It always seems higher, looking down from the top of an office building than it does looking up.)

I said I thought a waterfall there would be impressive. I suggested that he drive with me to the Calendar place, just a few minutes away, where, four years before, I had built a small waterfall just one-tenth as high as his would be. We went to Calendar's, where, by this time, the planting was mature. He saw the ten-foot waterfall, and he said, "Build mine, but make it as good as this."

We built it; it was successful. It certainly was a conversation piece for all of his guests, and he thoroughly enjoyed it.

In the 1920s the population of Beverly Hills was largely Caucasian-American, mostly Catholic and Protestant. It was part of a holiday ritual for all the homeowners to decorate their houses at Christmastime, and there was much rivalry to produce the most successful display. The week before Christmas, and the week after, droves of people traveled around every night, enjoying the displays.

When Harold Lloyd moved into his home, he outdid them all. He erected a huge Christmas tree at the top of the waterfall and decorated it as only a movie star would, with an impressive array of electric lights, hundreds of colored balls, and other traditional ornaments. The waterfall was turned on every night during the holidays and was flooded with multicolored lights.

Harold Lloyd certainly got his money's worth from that waterfall.

The Upper Ten Acres

In July 1925 Sumner Spaulding informed me that the Lloyds had chosen Italian Renaissance as the type of architecture for their home. He had shown them many photographs of different villas built between 1450 and 1550. The building that the Lloyds liked best was the palace of Cardinal Ferdinando de Medici in Rome, built in 1550.

I knew of few homes of Italian architecture in the Los Angeles area, and no Italian gardens. So, when Sumner Spaulding said it was to be of Italian Renaissance architecture, I made up my mind

to find out as much as I could about the Italian Renaissance villas, and what kind of dwellings and gardens they had. I acquired all the books available about Italian Renaissance architecture, which, of course, included Italian gardens.

I realized the Italian Renaissance garden required much more than the planting of some shrubs, trees, and flowers. I learned that the Renaissance garden was designed by the architect of the dwelling; that the garden was an integral part of the house; that the garden contained fountains, pools, cascades, garden houses, gazebos, stairways, balustrades, and much more.

Harold Lloyd was going to build an Italian Renaissance palace on the top of his hill, and I was determined to build gardens befitting his Italian home.

Under my arrangements with the Harold Lloyd Corporation, I was paid a set monthly fee. The

Harold Lloyd Garden, Beverly Hills, 1925–29. Construction starting at the bottom of what was to be the waterfall.

Harold Lloyd Garden, Beverly Hills, 1925–29. The completed waterfall, 100 feet high. The foreground is where it enters the canoe course. We built a number of those small bridges of Santa Susana sandstone. Just to the left of the top of the waterfall is our overlook rock.

Harold Lloyd Garden, Beverly Hills, 1925–29. A side view of the cutting-garden glass house and lath house. The trees in the background are on the neighboring property. The pile of sticks in the foreground is where the swimming pool would be built two years later.

amount of the fee was net to me. All costs of every kind for drafting, engineering, etc. were paid by the Harold Lloyd Corporation. In the previous months there had never been a question about how much I spent for professional services.

Movie producers hired, besides actors, the finest creative people in the world for their productions, and paid fabulous salaries—not only to writers and musicians, but to people who designed and built the sets. And, in those days, the sets for D. W. Griffith's *Birth of a Nation,* sets for Cecil B. DeMille, Samuel Goldwyn, and Douglas Fairbanks were very elaborate. None of these producers thought anything of building the sets, shooting the picture, and then tearing them down. Harold Lloyd produced his own movies—he was a producer himself.

When I looked over the plans Spaulding had given me, I knew I needed someone who was familiar with Italian Renaissance architecture. I needed a highly trained designer for my garden architecture—a top-notch man.

I talked to Spaulding on the phone and asked him if he knew where to find the kind of architectural draftsman I wanted. The next week he phoned and said he had made an appointment with Kenneth

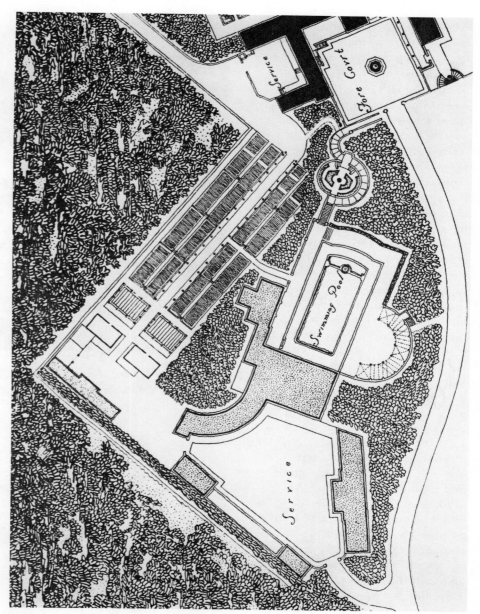

Harold Lloyd Garden, Beverly Hills, 1925–29. To the left of the word "Service" (in the lower left portion of the plan) are the dog kennels. The curved part of the building is the garage, with servants' rooms above, then a handball court, swimming pool, and dressing rooms. The upper part of the building is the recreational area. To the right of the word "Service" are potting sheds; then on the left more potting sheds, glass houses, lath houses, and the long, terraced cutting garden with the pergola through the middle. To the right of the upper end of the pergola is the stairway connecting the swimming pool and the forecourt. The circular part of the stairway is the landing.

Carpenter to go over the plans of the Harold Lloyd home. Carpenter was enthusiastic about Spaulding's plans. He had been head designer in a number of the leading ar-chitectural offices in the east and had designed homes for estates on Long Island and those gilded palaces for the multi-millionaires of Newport, Rhode Island. He had come to Southern California because of the climate. At the time of our lunch meeting, he was between jobs.

After lunch Carpenter and I went to the Lloyd property. I showed him the golf course and Joe Weston's old mill, and then we walked all over the upper ten acres. At the end of the afternoon I made him a financial proposition. It was very generous—more money than he could possibly get working for anybody else, because he was really working, through me, for Harold Lloyd, and Harold Lloyd was a producer. Carpenter accepted my proposition.

Carpenter and I went to work immediately. We spent days making various drawings of the landscaping, and when we arrived at our final landscape scheme for the Villa Medici dwelling, I submitted it to Harold Lloyd, who approved it.

We were able, in the spring of 1926, to do a considerable amount of grading on the upper ten acres, because we now knew the grade and location of the house. All grading in those days was done by teams of mules, or horses. Two animals are not a team; that's a pair. Several pairs make a team.

First the ground was plowed, and then the dirt was moved using a Fresno. A Fresno is very much the shape of a dustpan. This operation required two men. One man drove the animals. Those animals were motivated by means of a whip and language (not fit to print here) that they thoroughly understood, accompanied by much chewing of tobacco. The other man handled the plow or the Fresno.

Because the tennis court and the terminal of the formal garden were quite a distance from the location of the house, I could build those two structures before the house was completed without any danger of their being damaged.

I could also construct the end of the library garden. The construc-

Harold Lloyd Garden, Beverly Hills, 1925–29. A view of the swimming pool and the recreational building from the landing garden.

Harold Lloyd Garden, Beverly Hills, 1925–29. The swimming-pool complex shortly after it was completed. Harold Lloyd is in the foreground. Daughter Gloria is standing at the doorway of one of the dressing rooms. The next doorway led to the handball court. The recreation building contained a large rumpus room (or living room), a huge fireplace, completely equipped kitchen, and butler's pantry. Over a long period of years, this was probably the most popular and most used area of the entire estate.

Harold Lloyd Garden, Beverly Hills, 1925–29. A photograph taken as construction of the swimming pool was starting. In the foreground are Mrs. Lloyd, Harold Lloyd, and Gloria; in the background, Sumner Spaulding, architect; on the extreme left Mr. Edwards, contractor of the house and swimming pool. The other men are from Sumner Spaulding's office.

Harold Lloyd Garden, Beverly Hills, 1925–29. The steam shovel is beginning the excavation for the swimming pool. The trees in boxes are going to be used near the swimming pool.

Harold Lloyd Garden, Beverly Hills, 1925–29. Sumner Spaulding was the architect of the swimming pool and the swimming-pool building. The landscape architect designed and constructed all the remaining areas. All the trees have just been moved in.

Harold Lloyd Garden, Beverly Hills, 1925–29. The swimming pool area was reached by a stairway starting at the forecourt and descending to the level of the swimming pool itself. Halfway down, we had a landing.

tion was done in conformance with the landscape plan for Spaulding's Villa Medici-type of dwelling. We made rapid progress with the work.

And then, like a bolt out of the blue, Spaulding informed me that Harold Lloyd had changed his mind; he was not going to build a Roman Villa. He had decided that the Villa Medici project was too pretentious; he would be more comfortable with a Tuscany-type architecture. Of all the villas in the environs of Florence, Harold Lloyd liked best the Tuscany Villa

Gamberaia, built in 1610. The change in plans at this late date— the summer of 1926—was a great shock.

I clearly remember going with Harold Lloyd to Spaulding's office, where he was completing the working drawings on the Villa Gamberaia-type structure. That day Spaulding was studying whether to move the library windows six or eight inches, either up or down. Harold Lloyd was very disturbed.

When we were outside of Spaulding's office, Harold Lloyd

turned to me and said, "The only thing to do is to hit Spaulding on the head with a baseball bat, take the drawings away from him, and build the damn thing!" We had come to that very dangerous point where Mr. Moneybags—if he is very, very rich—can say, "To hell with it! I've lost all interest in it. We'll shut up the shop and write the loss off." And that would have been a terrific black eye for all of the professional people concerned.

The building of a home is almost always a joint project of both husband and wife, and many times they each have a different point of view, which can place the architect in a difficult position. He cannot take sides with either one.

The road to an architect's hell is paved with drawings of buildings that have never been built. What good are drawings if you don't build the structure? In a long, drawn-out construction project, it is absolutely imperative that the client be kept interested. Without the urge on his part to see something built, nothing ever happens.

I contacted Weber, Spaulding's senior partner, and we finally got action, so that construction on the house might begin.

By the end of 1926, I had to discontinue the landscaping because the construction of the house was progressing so slowly.

However, by the fall of 1927, the construction of the Villa Gamberaia-type house was well under way, and I was able to resume construction of the gardens in April 1928. The work moved rapidly; we were literally shoving the contractor out of our way. The gardens were completed just before the stock-market crash, October 1929.

Back in 1925 Spaulding and I had decided that the bridge over the canoe course was landscape architecture, but that the entrance-way walls, gate, and gatehouse (and the servants' quarters attached to it) were Spaulding's responsibility.

Harold Lloyd Garden, Beverly Hills, 1925–29. Looking from the terrace of the swimming pool to the landing garden. The flight of steps made a right angle turn; then additional steps led up to the bench of the landing garden.

Harold Lloyd Garden, Beverly Hills, 1925–29. At the landing, halfway between the forecourt and the swimming pool, we placed a bench, which offered a view of the landing garden and the swimming pool.

Unfortunately, Spaulding had not constructed these buildings before the stock-market crash, and they were never built. For the next forty years, the gatehouse was a six-foot by six-foot, board and batten structure—just room enough for the gateman. The gate was of rough redwood planking.

At the end of January 1930, I told the Harold Lloyd board of directors that they did not need to pay me a fee any longer.

On February first, I met *Mr.* Lloyd in his library, and I said, "Mr. Lloyd, I'm off your payroll, and I'm now going to call you Harold." And I called him Harold from that moment on, until he passed away in 1971. It was forty-one years of friendship.

The Tennis Court

Harold Lloyd wanted to night-light the tennis court so that he could play tennis in the evening. It's almost unbelievable, but the nearest night-lighted tennis court, according to the Southern California Edison Company, was at Riverside. (Now, you can't drive more than a few blocks from your front door without bumping into a night-lighted tennis court.)

The Edison Company made arrangements with the owner of that tennis court for Spaulding, Carpenter, Hampton (who was a clerk in the Harold Lloyd Corporation), and me to visit this home in Riverside. We arrived in the afternoon so we could see the tennis court in the daytime, had supper as guests of the Edison Company, and returned to the tennis court after dark, when the lights were turned on. It was a delightful house, and the wall of the living room facing the tennis court was of sliding glass doors, floor to ceiling. Again, this was very unusual at that time.

The Edison Company designed and built the night-lighting fixtures for Harold Lloyd's tennis court. Harold Lloyd was one of the top personalities in the world. Everyone would do anything to please him, and it was a terrific advertisement for any corporation to have its product used on the Harold Lloyd estate.

Harold Lloyd Garden, Beverly Hills, 1925–29. Opposite the entertainment pavilion was a circular pergola.

Harold Lloyd Garden, Beverly Hills, 1925–29. The wrought-iron gate opened onto a path, which crossed the driveway and led to the library garden.

Gloria's Play Yard

In the summer of 1927, when Harold Lloyd's daughter Gloria was three years old, I thought about what I would do if I were Harold Lloyd. If I had his money, I would build for Gloria a delightful fairyland for her very own. It would be something out of Mother Goose, or Cinderella, or Little Red Riding Hood. It would be a fairy-tale land.

I again contacted Joe Weston, who had designed the old mill on the golf course that was so pleasing to Harold Lloyd. I showed him the area we had reserved for a children's play yard.

I said, "Let's do an Elizabethan house and farmstead, but on the scale of a three-year-old child, rather than a six-foot adult. It would be a fairyland house."

I didn't have to do any urging or pushing; Joe was all enthusiasm. He made some watercolor sketches of a Mother Goose house with a thatched roof, an old well, a stable and carriage house combined, with an open archway through the mid-dle of it to a little paddock. Then, between the cottage and the stable, we would build a slide—not an ordinary slide, but one that had a curve to it.

The slide would be made of soapstone, which was used to make the drainboards of kitchen sinks. When it was highly waxed, it would have enough speed to give a youngster a thrill. But the sides would be high enough so that a three-year-old girl could not possibly fall off and get hurt. She would walk up the steep stairway to the platform on the top, which would have a roof topped with a weathervane of Old Father Time with his scythe.

I submitted Joe Weston's delightful watercolor sketches to Harold Lloyd. He okayed them and we started construction.

It was really a fairyland. Everybody working on it enjoyed it a great deal. Every manufacturer was delighted to have a finger in the pie. The advertising value of being able to say they had made the fixtures, or furnished the material, was tremendous. Gladding McBean, the ceramic tile manufacturer, was responsible for the delightful shingle-tile roof on the stables.

The thatched roof on Gloria's playhouse presented some difficulties. We had trouble finding the necessary supply of wheatstraw, but finally located some—35 miles away, at Thousand Oaks. It was a romantic touch of authenticity; however, we realized that unless we made it fireproof, it would be too hazardous. I had the available fire retardant treatments researched and chose the most effective spray on the market. We thatched the roof, satisfied that Gloria's playhouse would be safe.

The crossbeam had "Gloria" carved over the door, and at either side of her name were carvings of flowers. This main beam was supported by six carved heads, each one different. The walls of the house were of formally laid stone. The gable end was half-timber and plaster. The center ornament in the plaster was an old witch on a broomstick, crosssing in front of the moon. Below her, in the

Harold Lloyd Garden, Beverly Hills, 1925–29. The cutting-garden pergola has just been completed.

Harold Lloyd Garden, Beverly Hills, 1925–29. A view from the swimming-pool pergola. We really crowded the house construction crew. In 1925 this was a bare piece of land. We almost moved in the Forest of Arden. There were no tree movers, or people who made a business of supplying specimen trees, in 1925. The landscape architect had his own crew locating and buying trees and large shrubs from the yards of small bungalows.

plaster work, was a house, similar to Gloria's. The date 1927 was carved in the crossbeam immediately above the old witch.

Joe Weston designed every piece of the furniture. The bed was a four-poster, with side curtains. There was a baby's crib, with rockers. All of the furniture was Elizabethan in character. The plumbing fixtures were up-to-date, and built to scale.

The whole of this area was enclosed with a rough rubble wall, capped with flagstone. The gates into that dream world were a stroke of genius on Joe Weston's part. On the gateposts on either side were two brownies. It was a double gate that pivoted on hinges, so it always stayed closed. The brownies and the gate were made of one-half-inch solid brass, and a legend on the gates said, "Come into my garden and play."

I take no credit for the design of Gloria's play world, but I was the finger-pointer, the orchestra leader; if I had not thought of the idea and gotten Harold Lloyd to spend the money, it would never have been done.

Harold Lloyd Garden, Beverly Hills, 1925–29. The fountain was designed by the architect, Sumner Spaulding. One of the five pepper trees that were originally on the upper ten acres is shown at the left-hand edge of the photograph. The black streak on the roadway between the two entranceway posts is an iron grill, which picked up all the water from the forecourt.

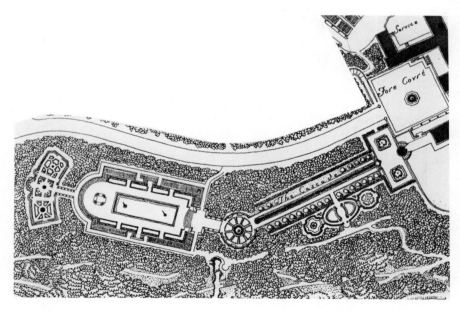

Harold Lloyd Garden, Beverly Hills, 1925–29. The presentation plot plan of the axial gardens southeast of the house. This drawing depicts the cascade, the baroque bulb garden, the "Medici" fountain, "Villa d'Este" lily pool, suntrap, and rose garden.

Harold Lloyd Garden, Beverly Hills, 1925–29. The forecourt side of the house. The pepper tree, which is one of the five originals, is being protected by a heavy wooden barrier. The house is reinforced concrete, of excellent workmanship and good architecture. Starting on the extreme right, a portion of the library loggia is shown, the opening of the forecourt, and its loggia.

Harold Lloyd Garden, Beverly Hills, 1925–29. The baroque bulb garden, showing the center section and the south end with its birdbath.

Harold Lloyd Garden, Beverly Hills, 1925–29. Harold Lloyd, picking kumquats just outside his library. This was the beginning of the cascade, which was terminated by a fountain patterned after the famous fountain in front of the Villa Medici in Rome. To the left of the fountain was the start of the waterfall.

Left: Harold Lloyd Garden, Beverly Hills, 1925–29. Harold Lloyd's library, taken a few weeks after the family had moved into their new house. Practically every room in the house had two or three bouquets of flowers, all from the estate's cutting garden. The garden cascade began just outside of the French doors.

Harold Lloyd Garden, Beverly Hills, 1925–29. The beginning of the water cascade. The archway in the background is the entrance to Harold Lloyd's library. The two large trees on either side of the archway are Pittosporum undulatum, *moved in full-grown. The many varieties of* Pittosporum, *which is native mostly to Australia, have since the late nineteenth century been used extensively in California. Because of their ease of growth, they have been used for both hedges and small trees. This photograph was taken approximately two years after the garden was completed.*

Harold Lloyd Garden, Beverly Hills, 1925–29. The start of the cascade, photographed just after the planting was finished. A lamp is shown next to the first three cypresses on the left-hand side. So many of these lamps were used on the estate that you could read a newspaper anywhere at night. In addition to being ornamental, they were used for security reasons.

Harold Lloyd Garden, Beverly Hills, 1925–29. The end of the cascade.

Harold Lloyd Garden, Beverly Hills, 1925–29. The start of the cascade; the loggia in the background is off Harold Lloyd's library (photograph: 1974).

Harold Lloyd Garden, Beverly Hills, 1925–29. The "Villa Medici" Fountain, 1929. The white, black, red, and brown pebbles of the pavement were obtained by our crew on the seashore near San Diego. We worked the design "H L" into one of the segments of paving.

Harold Lloyd Garden, Beverly Hills, 1925–29. The start of the cascade, bordered by Italian cypress (photograph: 1971).

Harold Lloyd Garden, Beverly Hills, 1925–29. A view from the bottom of the cascade to the loggia of the library. We were planting under difficult conditions, but we were determined to go as fast as we possibly could. It was almost three and one-half years from the time we started the golf course until this photograph was taken.

Harold Lloyd Garden, Beverly Hills, 1925–29. Construction of the library garden was interrupted by the construction of the house. Eighteen months after we began the library garden, we were able to resume, and this photograph is a view from the unfinished loggia of Harold Lloyd's library. The cascade's basins are just being constructed.

Harold Lloyd Garden, Beverly Hills, 1925–29. We made a mock-up of the "Villa Medici" fountain, to be sure that the proportions of the fountain-to-be were correct. Often it is difficult to judge from a drawing.

Left: Harold Lloyd Garden, Beverly Hills, 1925–29. The water is dripping cleanly from the upper basin, not flowing on the undersurface of the basin. We found that cutting a bead or a groove underneath the lip would make the water drop cleanly (photograph: 1974).

Harold Lloyd Garden, Beverly Hills, 1925–29. View of the cascade from the "Villa Medici" fountain.

Harold Lloyd Garden, Beverly Hills, 1925–29. The "Villa d'Este" pool, with its suntrap. The suntrap is the terminal of the library garden. This photograph was taken from the "Villa Medici" fountain at the end of the cascade. The pool is located four feet below the fountain. Two years prior to the construction of this suntrap, I had made a playhouse for a client whose young daughter was in poor health. I had read about glass that would admit the violet rays of the sun. It had a therapeutic effect. You could get a slight suntan. So, when we built the suntrap, we glazed three sides of it with that type of glass. The side that faced toward the cascade was open.

Harold Lloyd Garden, Beverly Hills, 1925–29. Construction of one of the terrace walls.

Harold Lloyd Garden, Beverly Hills, 1925–29. Construction of the "Villa d'Este" pool and the suntrap was begun in July 1926, and in this photograph the construction is almost finished—three and one-half months of work.

Right, above: Harold Lloyd Garden, Beverly Hills, 1925–29. A view from the suntrap, looking toward the "Villa Medici" fountain. This pool was inspired by Maxfield Parrish's painting of the Villa d'Este gardens at Tivoli. Not included is the nude girl that Maxfield Parrish had in his painting.

Right: Harold Lloyd Garden, Beverly Hills, 1925–29. We used pots, and more pots! The six large pots shown in the foreground were the standard pots we had made for the Harold Lloyd estate. The molds for the pots were ours, and no one else was supposed to use them.

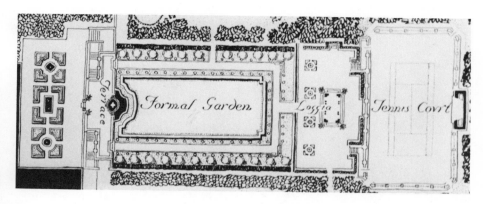

Harold Lloyd Garden, Beverly Hills, 1925–29. The presentation drawing of the plot plan of the principal formal garden.

Harold Lloyd Garden, Beverly Hills, 1925–29. View of the dining-room terrace retaining wall, the steps leading to the "Palladian"-pavilion formal garden, and the fountain that was the starting point of that formal garden.

Harold Lloyd Garden, Beverly Hills, 1925–29. The presentation plot plan of the rose garden.

Harold Lloyd Garden, Beverly Hills, 1925–29. Double flight of steps from the dining-room terrace, leading to the "Palladian"-pavilion formal garden. The design of these steps was influenced by the garden steps at the Villa Gamberaia.

Left: Harold Lloyd Garden, Beverly Hills, 1925–29. The "Palladian" pavilion (terminal building) a year after its completion. In the lower right-hand corner is a geometric pattern of English boxwood. We designed the furniture, which was executed by a shop, 75 percent of whose production was for my gardens.

Right: Harold Lloyd Garden, Beverly Hills, 1925–29. Looking through the "Palladian" pavilion to the wall of the dining-room terrace garden. The opening in the wall led into the basement. On the left of that opening is the 55,000-gallon water-storage reservoir.

Harold Lloyd Garden, Beverly Hills, 1925–29. A view of the "Palladian"-pavilion formal garden. The fountain is the start of the formal garden; the "Palladian" pavilion is its terminal. On either side, and at the end of the rectangular bowling green, are paths lined on all sides by rows of dwarf citrus in terra-cotta pots on octagonal, cast-stone bases. This arrangement of potted plants was often employed in Italian Renaissance gardens. At the time we made this garden, I had never seen this arrangement used in any gardens in America.

Harold Lloyd Garden, Beverly Hills, 1925–29. For a few years conducted tours were taken through the estate. Later, it was occasionally used as the locale of television sequences. The two people in the pavilion are actors.

Harold Lloyd Garden, Beverly Hills, 1925–29. Another view of the ''Palladian''-pavilion formal garden.

Harold Lloyd Garden, Beverly Hills, 1925–29. A watercolor sketch of the proposed wall fountain, which was to be the terminal of the vista from the west door of the living room. This fountain was not built because of the stock-market crash of 1929.

Harold Lloyd Garden, Beverly Hills, 1925–29. The parapet wall was built by Sumner Spaulding. The two upright columns were copied from those at the Villa Mondrogone in Italy. These columns served as smokestacks for the barroom below. The surrounding trees are California oaks that had just been moved in and planted.

Left: Harold Lloyd Garden, Beverly Hills, 1925–29. The northerly facade of the house. The first two French doors lead into the living room; the next two smaller doors enter Mrs. Lloyd's music room. Thousands of flowering plants in pots were used on the estate. Those in bloom here were cineraria.

Right: Harold Lloyd Garden, Beverly Hills, 1925–29. This photograph (dated September 12, 1926) is interesting historically in that it shows how concrete tennis courts were constructed at that time. One can see the extensive amount of reinforcing steel that was placed in the concrete slab. The electric lights strung across the court—on a level with the architectural balls of the fencing—were necessary because the cement slab was poured after dark; otherwise, it would have dried out too fast during the pouring. The concrete had to be poured continuously.

Harold Lloyd Garden, Beverly Hills, 1925–29. A view of the tennis court, taken from the pavilion. The panel at the rear of the spectator's building is glazed tile.

51

Harold Lloyd Garden, Beverly Hills, 1925–29. The plot plan of the children's garden.

Harold Lloyd Garden, Beverly Hills, 1925–29. Gloria's farmstead nearing completion. One can see the large size of the trees that were moved onto the site.

Harold Lloyd Garden, Beverly Hills, 1925–29. The entranceway to Gloria's farmstead, built in 1927 (photograph: 1975).

Right: Harold Lloyd Garden, Beverly Hills, 1925–29. A photograph taken immediately after the completion of the slide. There's Old Father Time as a weathervane, and a cuckoo clock. On the top of the steeple is an ornament of the cow jumping over the moon.

Harold Lloyd Garden, Beverly Hills, 1925–29. A photograph taken in 1928, just after Gloria's farmstead had been completed. All the trees were moved in full-grown. You can see the date (1927) on the crossbeams of the dwelling.

Left: Harold Lloyd Garden, Beverly Hills, 1925–29. Three-year-old Gloria in the doorway of her very own house. The windows on either side of the door are authentic roundel windows.

Harold Lloyd Garden, Beverly Hills, 1925–29. Gloria's stable and carriage house, just after it was completed. The small tile on the steeple was specially made for the stable. Fantail pigeons were kept in the pigeon loft. The pony stall had Dutch doors so the pony could look out. The archway led to a monkey house and an aviary.

The Henry Kern Garden
Holmby Hills
1925

From a news item I found that Mr. and Mrs. Henry Kern were building a new home of Italian Renaissance architecture in Holmby Hills. I phoned Mr. Kern and told him of the work I was doing on the Harold Lloyd estate (which he could see from his homesite), and that I would like to be his landscape architect. I met the Kerns at their new home the next day and explained to Mr. Kern that, like his architect, I worked on a fee basis. That was agreeable to him, and after he had done some checking up on me, I became his landscape architect. The architect of the house was George Washington Smith of Santa Barbara, and his good right arm and designer was

Henry Kern Garden, Holmby Hills, 1925. A view of the west garden and the cascade shortly after completion (from The Architect, *Vol. 10, August, 1928).*

Lutah Maria Riggs. Miss Riggs visited the Kern job once a week to check on its progress, and she and I became friends.

The Kerns were not local people. They had come from the East Coast to escape the severe winters. Mr. Kern had just retired from active business. He had plenty of money but was careful with it. However, Mr. Kern was not penny-pinching when it came to his family life. He wanted to have the very best kind of environment. The Kerns were typical of a certain class of affluent people who had discovered Southern California, and particularly Los Angeles, after World War I.

The Kerns' house was on the top of a knoll, with an uninterrupted view of the Santa Monica coastline. The garden facade of the house, which was mainly a loggia, faced west. Sixty feet from the loggia, where the land sloped steeply downhill, we constructed a balustrade. In the center we built a fountain, which was the source of the water for the cascade we constructed down the slope. The cascade was terminated with a pool.

Between the balustrade and the house we made a formal garden. The main pathway of the formal garden was lined with dwarf orange trees in pots set on concrete bases, typical of Italian Renaissance gardens.

When I was almost finished with the garden, Mr. Kern decided that he would like to have some garden statuary. He had heard of Marshall Laird, a very canny Scotsman who dealt in fine furniture and various art objects, including garden statuary. Mr. and Mrs. Kern and I went to Marshall Laird's establishment to see what he had. Mr. Kern took along his father-in-law, who was born in the old country, spoke with an accent, and had made his money the hard, slow way with a dairy lunch restaurant in downtown Manhattan.

Henry Kern Garden, Holmby Hills, 1925. The fountain at the top of the cascade. The pool below the fountain fed water to the cascade (from The Architect, *Vol. 10, August, 1928).*

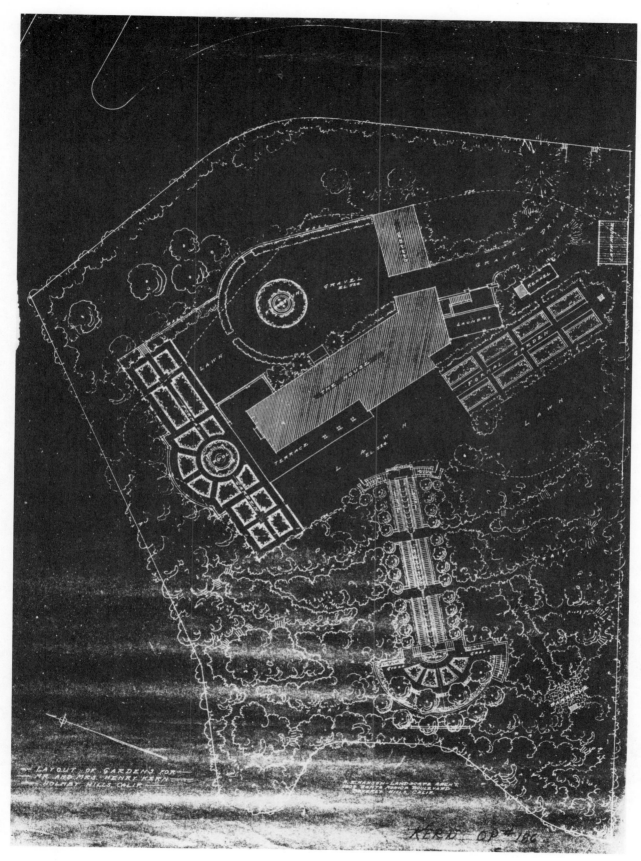

Kern Garden, Holmby Hills, 1925. Plot plan of the garden.

Mr. Kern picked out a quantity of merchandise, not only garden pieces, but various pieces of furniture for the house. He would turn to his wife each time to say, "Isn't it lovely? Isn't it nice? It will fit in."

The Italian garden pieces that they chose were just right for the garden. The bill was totaled and amounted to $6,000. Mr. Kern said, "Now, what's the wholesale price?"

Marshall Laird said, "That is the wholesale price."

Mr. Kern was a little irked, but he liked the items he had chosen. He said, "I pay cash, so what's the cash discount?"

And this is the pay-off: Marshall Laird said, "No discount, but I'll deliver it free."

Mr. Kern's father-in-law poked his elbow into my ribs and said, "———the damn fool! If he wants to buy it cheap, he shouldn't like it!"

And that was another lesson.

Henry Kern Garden, Holmby Hills, 1925. The upper section of the cascade with one of the two stairs leading from the garden terrace (from The Architect, *Vol. 10, August, 1928).*

Kern Garden, Holmby Hills, 1925. Garden facade of the house and the cascade. The photograph was taken just months after completion.

The George I. Cochran Garden
Los Angeles
1928

In the late spring of 1928, Mrs. George I. Cochran phoned to discuss the landscaping of their property. The Cochrans proved to be the right kind of client for my walled garden! Mr. Cochran was the head of the Pacific Mutual Life Insurance Company. He knew of me because I had done a small garden for the Pacific Mutual Life Insurance building in downtown Los Angeles.

The Cochran house, on the west side of Harvard, was old, well built, and comfortable. Mr. Cochran had acquired the property on Harvard on either side of his home and had also acquired all of the adjoining houses and lots on Hobart, which backed up to his

home. That way, he was assured of privacy.

When I met with the Cochrans, I spent considerable time explaining the idea of doing a completely walled-in garden like the smaller gardens in Versailles. I knew that money wasn't going to be any hurdle as long as the Cochrans could have a garden that they would really enjoy. They were dignified, sophisticated people—I believe somewhere in their late sixties.

Mr. and Mrs. Cochran were interested in the kind of landscaping that I proposed, and they commissioned me to make some sketches. Lee Rombotis, my head designer, had been trained at the Beaux Arts and had been to Versailles a

number of times. The morning following my first visit with the Cochrans, I explained to Lee Rombotis what I had in mind and had him make a number of rough sketches of different garden schemes. I selected one I thought would be appropriate for the Cochrans and had a garden plot plan made of it, as well as a cross section. Mr. and Mrs. Cochran liked what I suggested and authorized further studies.

After my designer had made a number of plans, I selected one I thought would be ideal for the Cochrans and had a model made of it. When the model was completed, I phoned Mrs. Cochran and said I would like to meet with

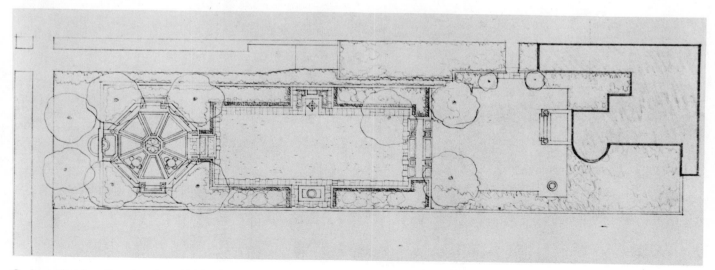

Cochran Garden, Los Angeles, 1928. Garden plan submitted, approved, and built. The total dimension of the principal garden was 56 feet by 202 feet.

59

them at their home. I didn't want them to come to the office. I was going to take the model to their home, sit down with them in Mr. Cochran's favorite sunroom, place the model in front of them, and show them my dreams.

I took the model to the Cochran's sunroom. After I had set up a piano stool and the model, I had Mrs. Cochran and then Mr. Cochran look through a powerful reading glass at the model. The reading glass magnified the scale, and sitting in the sunroom looking at the model, they could see the garden as it was to be.

I told the Cochrans of the various materials that would be used in the garden. I said it was going to be expensive, but that I knew they would thoroughly enjoy living in it. It would be like nothing else that I knew of in California.

At the end of the afternoon, they employed me to build the garden.

Cochran Garden, Los Angeles, 1928. Looking from the terminal of the garden toward the house. The grass panel is 27 feet wide, 80 feet long. This photograph was taken a few weeks after the garden was completed. All trees shown were moved in full-grown.

Cochran Garden, Los Angeles, 1928. Close-up of the wall fountain. It is truly garden architecture—very few plants. This wall fountain gave a strong vertical dimension to the garden.

Cochran Garden, Los Angeles, 1928. The sundial and the entranceway to the garage from the garden, north wall of the property.

Cochran Garden, Los Angeles, 1928. The birdbath and the decorative panel of the south wall of the garden. The photograph clearly shows that the garden was more than just plants; it was garden architecture.

Cochran Garden, Los Angeles, 1928. Detail of the floor of the octagonal platform. The table in the lower right-hand corner was specially made for this garden. All of the stonework was of Tuffa stone, very carefully executed.

Cochran Garden, Los Angeles, 1928. The door leading from the garden to the service area. The two pots are imported Italian pieces; the trees are kumquats.

Above: Cochran Garden, Los Angeles, 1928. Looking from the terminal of the garden toward the house. The grass panel is 27 feet wide, 80 feet long. This photograph was taken a few weeks after the garden was completed. All trees shown were moved in full grown.

Below: Cochran Garden, Los Angeles, 1928. A rendering of the cross section of the garden. This rendering was submitted before any work had been started, and in some ways more clearly shows what the garden was like when completed than the photographs. The two trees on the left are live oaks, accurately shown as to size— moved in full-grown. The two trees on the right, Pittosporum undulatum, *were also fully grown when moved in.*

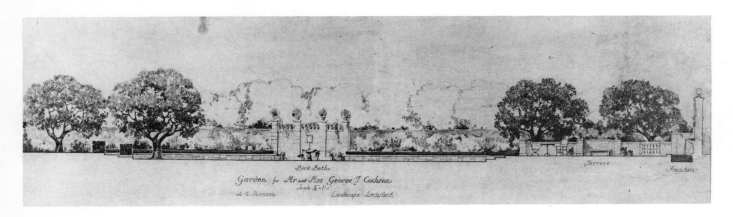

The Lockhart Garden
Los Angeles
1928

In the spring of 1928, Joe Weston phoned me. (He was the architect who did the old mill golf house on the Harold Lloyd estate, and that darling Gloria Lloyd fairyland). He said he was remodeling a house at the southwest corner of Irving and Sixth Street, and he wanted me to do the landscaping.

I met with Weston on the property, and he introduced me to Mr. and Mrs. Lockhart. Mr. Lockhart was president of the Rio Grande Oil Company—black gold, again. The Lockharts were tennis enthusiasts, so they bought the lot immediately behind their house for a tennis court.

The Lockhart house (now the official residence of the mayor of Los Angeles) was good architecture, modified Elizabethan. Weston had remodeled the interior so that when you entered the front door, you were in a two-story hall. In the back of the hall he put in some large French doors leading to a terrace.

Once I had finished the landscaping, you stepped down from the terrace to a rectangular lawn panel, hedged on each side with boxwood, eighteen inches high, then a six-foot-wide flower garden, and then an eight-foot hedge of *Eugenia myrtifolia.* In the flower garden I planted full-grown *Pit-*

tosporum undulatum trees, thirty feet apart. This formal garden was terminated by a garden house of the same architecture as the small houses in the vicinity of Broadway, England.

When you walked down the lawn panel and were almost to the garden house, you got a surprise—a sunken formal garden, crosswise to the lawn panel, patterned after the famous garden at Hampton Court in London.

Beyond the garden house was the tennis court. Between the tennis court and the sidewalk on Lorraine Street, we planted four very large redwood trees.

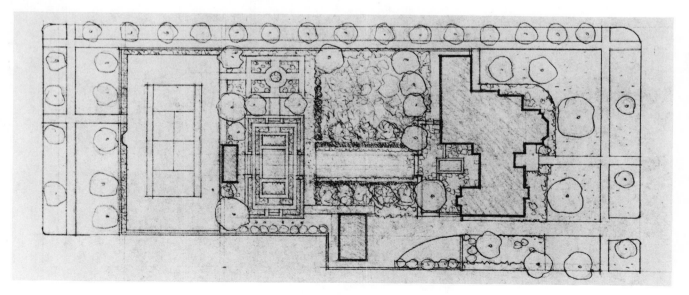

Lockhart Garden, Los Angeles, 1928. Plot plan of the garden (drawn in 1978 by illustrator Leavitt Dudley, as remembered by the author).

Lockhart Garden, Los Angeles, 1928. The terrace in the foreground was designed by architect Joe Weston. The flagstone paving was laid by the land-scape architect's crew. A simple but ef-fective garden. The rectangular lawn panel is one foot lower than the flagstone terrace. It is given distance, first by the two cone-shaped boxwoods in pots, then by the low wall, on which are two globe-shaped boxwoods in pots. At the very end of the lawn are two lead figures on pedestals. All of these details give distance by interrupting the view. The lawn panel is lined with flagstone walks on either side, then a flowerbed, then a low hedge one foot higher, then by large Pittosporum undulatum *bounded by a hedge of* Eugenia myrtifolia. *The slate-roofed garden-terminal building is of formally laid, rough-cut stone.*

Lockhart Garden, Los Angeles, 1928. A view of the sunken garden.

Lockhart Garden, Los Angeles, 1928. Photographed in 1928, just after the landscaping was completed. The plant-ing at the front is very simple; the en-trance is flanked by two fine specimens of Eugenia myrtifolia. *In the upper right-hand corner is the foliage of one of the largest live oaks we moved.*

Lockhart Garden, Los Angeles, 1928. The garden pavilion.

Lockhart Garden, Los Angeles, 1928. A view of the sunken garden. The fencing of the tennis court was quite elaborate, not at all routine. The terminal garden pavilion, which included a bar and toilet facilities, leads into the tennis court.

Lockhart Garden, Los Angeles, 1928. View looking from the sunken garden toward the house. The large tree in the background, Pittosporum undulatum, *has just been moved in. One of the lead figures on the pedestal is shown above the steps leading to the sunken garden.*

The Johnson Garden
Montecito
1928-29

In 1927 I had done a garden for Mr. and Mrs. Henry Kern on a knoll one street west of the Harold Lloyd estate. The architect for the Kern home was George Washington Smith of Santa Barbara. Mr. Kern had told Mr. Smith how well pleased he and Mrs. Kern were with the garden I had designed. In the early part of 1928, I received a telephone call from George Washington Smith, whom I had never met, asking me if I would come to his office in Montecito the next day. He was completing the construction of a home and wanted to discuss its landscaping with me. I was delighted.

Mr. Smith's office was on the grounds of his home. The drafting room faced north; outside of it was a unique garden, similar to those I had seen in Andalusian Spain.

On my arrival Mr. Smith explained to me that he was just completing a home for Mr. and Mrs. Kirk B. Johnson, a Tuscan villa somewhat similar to the architecture of the Villa Gamberaia in the environs of Florence.

Mr. and Mrs. Johnson had lived for a number of years in a large home in Beverly Hills. Wanting to get out of the hurly-burly life of the city, they had purchased twelve acres, five minutes away from George Washington Smith's office.

Mr. Smith drove me to the Johnson property. It consisted of eight acres on the flat, along Sycamore Canyon Road. There were four acres in a slope, at the bottom of which was Montecito Creek. This arroyo slope was covered with magnificent live oaks and luxuriant native shrubs.

The eight-acre site originally had had an old home on it, built in the 1880s. Mr. Smith tore this home down and built the Tuscan villa on its site. The Johnson home was nearly completed.

All of the Johnson property was a landscape architect's dream. There were magnificent live oaks and tremendous Monterey cypress planted many years earlier. No landscape architect could claim

Johnson Garden, Montecito, 1928–29. The formal entrance to the Kirk B. Johnson estate. George Washington Smith's architectural office designed the gateposts. The entrance drive is walled by mature Pittosporum undulatum. *The edging of the driveway is a cast-stone curb and gutter, which strongly delineate the driveway. The fountainhead of the pool is silhouetted against the dark color of the entrance door. The shadows (not shade) of the trees in the driveway add a dimension all their own (photograph: 1978).*

credit for the wonderful trees on the estate. They were God's gift to mankind. To say that I was thrilled is an understatement.

Mr. Smith turned me loose to wander around on my own. That same day he introduced me to Mr. and Mrs. Johnson. I always tried to visualize myself in the client's shoes, and I asked myself how I would like to have the home landscaped if I were Mr. Client. I never visualized doing a garden for the lady, but always for the man.

In 1928 fine homes in Santa Barbara and the vicinity were nearly always built for mature people of entrenched wealth. A great deal of it was second- and third-generation money. The men and women played golf; a number of the men played polo. Most of the people building new homes in Montecito and Santa Barbara had spent some time traveling abroad.

The Johnsons were typical of this leisure class. Mrs. Johnson had inherited the money, and I was told (not by Mr. Smith) that she was one of the five richest heiresses in the United States. Amongst other business ventures, her father had financed King C. Gillette, the safety razor man, and in doing so had made a lot of money. Mr. Johnson's only business that I knew of was handling Mrs. Johnson's money.

I would judge that the Johnsons were somewhere in their early sixties. They had no children. They didn't want a tennis court, kept their horses at a boarding stable, didn't want a swimming pool. So, it came down to building gardens to complement the Johnson villa.

While the exterior of the home was inspired by a seventeenth-century villa, the interior was as modern as tomorrow. I could tell the Johnsons were not the kind of people who would like to putter in a garden. They would like flowers only because they would add to the

Johnson Garden, Montecito, 1928–29. The presentation plot plan.

beauty of the grounds, and, when cut, would be an adornment to the interior. The Johnsons were ultrasophisticated and complicated. They were high society, with a capital "H."

The first thing I did when Mr. Smith turned me loose was to explore the first floor of the house. The front hall opened onto a loggia, beyond which there was a patio. This front hall was bisected by a long hall of narrower width. I turned right, into this hall. On the left was the drawing room, on the right the library. At the end of the hall were high French doors that opened onto a landing about three feet above the ground, with a double staircase to the ground. The other end of this hall terminated at the dining room, but before one got there, there was a door on the right leading to the owners' bedroom suite.

I now had the plan of the first floor in my mind, and I spent the balance of the afternoon walking all over the upper eight acres. What a treat the land was! I could do the landscaping without much grading. I didn't need to move a tree; I could use every one of them where it was. How different this was from all the gardens I had been landscaping in the Los Angeles area. Santa Barbara has one of the finest growing climates in the world—fertile soil, and, very important, soft water. We were not going to have to fight mineral salts in the soil and on the leaves of the plants.

In the late afternoon I went back to Mr. Smith's office. I had met Lutah Riggs, Mr. Smith's designer, on the Kern job, and I now renewed my acquaintance with her. A trained architect and a graduate of the University of California, Berkeley, she was indispensable to Mr. Smith. Miss Riggs supplied me with a contour map, the first-floor plan, and the elevations of the home. I don't know how I got back to Beverly

Johnson Garden, Montecito, 1928–29. The west auto forecourt. The flagstone paving around the center pool emphasizes the form of the fountain. On the left the forecourt is framed with a low wall, at the base of which are symmetrically cut flagstones. The two cypress trees probably date from 1880. The planting on the left was done in 1929 (photograph: 1978).

Johnson Garden, Montecito, 1928–29. A view of the auto forecourt. The design of the sides of the pool is taken from a fountain in Florence. The three cone-shaped objects that are the nozzle of the fountain are patterned after Italian beehives. This beehive fountainhead is taken from the fountain in the Villa Lanti.

Johnson Garden, Montecito, 1928–29. A detail of the loggia off the front entrance. Note that the foliage of the planted pots is consistently of the same form. The stone of the paving came from a local quarry and was cut and laid by the landscape architect's crew.

71

Hills, but I did—and safely. All the time I was pinching myself to see if what I was dreaming about was real. Was it true that there was a George Washington Smith, architect, and that there were Mr. and Mrs. Johnson, and did that magnificent piece of land actually exist?

Early next morning I was in my drafting room, making a rough layout of the landscaping for the estate, which broke itself into a number of sections: the entranceway and forecourt; the loggia and patio, facing east; the south area, viewed from the drawing room and the library; and the north area, viewed from the dining room.

The entrance road would lead straight to the front door. The forecourt would be ample, present-

Right: Johnson Garden, Montecito, 1928–29. A view of the loggia from the patio. The floor of the patio is of the same material used for the floor of the loggia. The umbrella table and chairs were designed by the landscape architect's office and were very similar to the furniture used at the Harold Lloyd estate.

Johnson Garden, Montecito, 1928–29. The one-story wing of the house is the owner's bedroom suite. On the right-hand side of the photograph is the parterre garden, photographed when it was fifty years old. The circle with the statue of ''Diana'' echoes the curved steps. At the end, the balustrade with the ball-topped pedestals makes a definite ending for the garden; it terminates it. The tall eucalyptus on the right helps to frame the view. The light grey mountains in the background are those of the coast range.

ing no problem for turning cars or for parking. There were two very large old cypresses in this forecourt area. In the middle I made a dot—for a pool. From the entranceway to the forecourt I would plant large shrubs on either side, so that when you entered from Sycamore Canyon Road, the effect would be almost that of a green tunnel. You would then see the low forecourt pool, with its ornamental spout and its stream of water—and then, the front door.

From the entrance hall you had a view of the loggia and the patio, which faced east. From the draw-

ing room and the library there was a view of a large, run-down Bermuda lawn, dotted with fine old trees. At the opposite end of the long hall was the dining room, and Mr. Smith had built, outside of this dining room, a small paved area with a pool. When you stood in the dining room and looked across the small, paved terrace, the ground rose very gently for some feet and then sloped downhill for a short distance. The view from this dining-room terrace was the very essence of Montecito: there were beautiful native oaks in the foreground, framing the view of

the mountains, which were, due to the distance, a light, bluish-grey—a fine contrast with the dark green oaks in the immediate foreground. It was like a Maxfield Parrish painting.

Five days after my visit with George Washington Smith on the Kirk B. Johnson grounds, I took Mr. Smith a rough sketch of my plans for the landscaping of the estate. He was pleased with it and asked me to make a more detailed rendering so that he could go over it with the Johnsons. A week later I returned to Montecito; after Mr. Smith, in my presence, went over

Johnson Garden, Montecito, 1928–29. View of the parterre garden. The pedestal with the ball finial makes a definite start for the garden, and the balustrade in the background makes a strong line of ending. Mr. and Mrs. Donahue, who acquired the property in the 1960s, kept it in immaculate condition. The statue of Diana in the middle of the parterre came from Mrs. Donahue's mother's (Mrs. Dan Murphy's) garden in Los Angeles. There is not a leaf or a footprint on the crushed-rock floor of the garden (photograph: 1978).

the landscaping plan with Mr. and Mrs. Johnson, they authorized me to proceed.

Mr. Smith knew of my method of operation from his conversations with the Henry Kerns, and he explained it to the Johnsons. I would make the drawings and construct the gardens myself. It would not be necessary to let the work out to a landscape contractor. I would receive a net fee of 15 percent of the total cost of the job, while all costs of every kind would be charged to the Johnsons. This was an unusual arrangement; the landscape architects I knew of charged a fee of 10 percent of the cost of the job, and they, in turn, put the work out for bid to landscape contractors, who made a substantial profit on the work.

No budget was made for the cost of the work, which was so varied that figuring the cost in advance

Right: Johnson Garden, Montecito, 1928–29. From the end of the parterre garden, a long walk terminated in a glass garden-gazing ball. In the middle of this long walk was a pergola.

Johnson Garden, Montecito, 1928–29. The planting at the right-hand edge of this photograph has matured as planned, effectively screening the English lawn that lies beyond. The pergola was lovely when the purple wisteria was in bloom. At the end of this pergola walk is a marble Roman god, placed there by the Donahues (photograph: 1978).

would have been difficult to do. On the other hand, George Washington Smith and the Johnsons had complete control over the expenditures, because they could have stopped the work any day and paid me my fee for what had been done up to that point. Again, this was an unusual arrangement, but these were unusual times. George Washington Smith's clients were extremely wealthy and could buy any toys they wanted. But the toys (in this case, landscaping) had to be unusual and good.

After I had received an okay from Mr. Johnson and from George Washington Smith, I went back to my office and real work began. I had to do two things: to get the working drawings going and complete the plan with my drafting staff, and to set up a construction organization. By the spring of 1928, I had a mature, well-run organization. We were used to doing out-of-town jobs, some as far away as San Diego. I went to Andy Anderson, my very competent superintendent on the

Harold Lloyd job, to discuss the construction of the Johnson gardens. Andy and I had been working together for more than three years, and we had good rapport.

I had Bob Smith, second in charge under Andy on the Lloyd job, in mind for the construction superintendent of the Johnson gardens, but he was working on the Harold Lloyd estate, and I hesitated to ask Andy to let him go. However, Andy, of his own free will, suggested that we take

Johnson Garden, Montecito, 1928–29. A view of the interior of the pergola, fifty years after it was constructed. The floor is of common red brick, laid in sand. No mortar was used (photograph: 1978).

Bob Smith. He had a great deal of construction background, having been a carpenter foreman, and he was used to our system of organization and method of work. Andy and I decided that we'd put him on the Johnson job.

Right: Johnson Garden, Montecito, 1928–29. The termination of the long pergola walk. The stock-market crash had just taken place, and an inexpensive glass garden-gazing ball, purchased for about $15, is in the center of the Maltese cross, where an expensive antique statue was originally planned.

Johnson Garden, Montecito, 1928–29. A close-up of the Maltese cross. After fifty years there is not a crack in the paving (photograph: 1978).

Johnson Garden, Montecito, 1928–29. The mosaic Maltese cross floor is of pebbles. The parterre is English boxwood—not Japanese—and was fifty years old (see photograph, upper left, for earlier view) when this photograph was taken (photograph 1978).

It was a happy choice. We worked on the job constantly from then until December 1929. The total area of the Johnson property was twelve acres, but the land we were going to develop immediately was eight acres—compared to the sixteen acres of Harold Lloyd's estate, just half the size. Probably one-tenth the problems.

When I began developing the working drawings, the Johnson home was completed except for some minor interior work; the family was almost ready to move in. The land was level, and I didn't have to worry about change of grades. We could go ahead full blast.

Plant material was no problem whatsoever. Santa Barbara had a number of fine nurseries—probably as fine as could be found anywhere in the world. The availability of plant material was unlimited. The necessary stone was also readily available. For many years there had been a group of master Italian stonemasons in the vicinity of Santa Barbara, and we had no problem obtaining stone or having it cut; they knew exactly what to do.

We had become acquainted with all the material dealers and suppliers. We knew where to buy lumber, where to buy cement, where to buy pipe, sand, and gravel, where to find flagstone—where to find all the unlimited amount of material and personnel it takes to make a great garden. No time was lost in starting work on the job. We didn't have to wait for working drawings, because there was a terrific amount of clean-up work and ground preparation to be done.

The Johnson gardens were garden architecture in the best sense of the word. I'd had a great deal of experience in doing small and medium-sized formal gardens, and the Johnsons', in a way, was a collection of formal gardens. None of those in the past, however, had been as important as this one.

Johnson Garden, Montecito, 1928–29. The terminal of the long south walk. The walk is wide enough to allow two or three people to walk abreast. The concrete edging delineates the strong line of the walk. The edging is an example of the "architecture" aspect of landscape architecture. If the walk were edged with shrubs or ground cover, the line would be weak. The oak in the foreground frames the view. The walk is in shadow—not shade. There's a difference; shadow has a pattern. The fountain is of white marble.

In a month we had finished intricate drawings for all of the property. We had to plan for every foot of grade, for drainage of the land, and for the handling of surface water. Although we don't have much rain in Southern California, when it does rain, it comes down quite heavily, and the volume of flow is large. We had to

77

be sure that our paths were graded so that they wouldn't be washed out in a heavy rain. A tremendous amount of work and engineering goes into creating a garden of the kind we were constructing for the Johnsons. We were able to do the work gradually, and to do it well. Over a long period of years there has been no problem in taking care of the storm water.

No landscape architect can take the credit for the beauty of the grounds of the Kirk B. Johnson estate. Time and Mother Nature did the job.

Johnson Garden, Montecito, 1928–29. The southern east-west alley (photograph: 1978).

Johnson Garden, Montecito, 1928–29. The fountain terminal of the long south walk. The background wall is Pittosporum undulatum. *The low edgings are Japanese boxwood. The statuary was placed there by Mr. and Mrs. Donahue.*

Johnson Garden, Montecito, 1928–29. This lovely little temple was originally in the Dan Murphy garden in Los Angeles and was later placed in the rose garden of the Kirk B. Johnson estate (photograph: 1978).

Left: Johnson Garden, Montecito, 1928–29. The "English" south lawn, terminated by another marble statue. The magnificent high blue gums (Eucalyptus globulus) add a vertical dimension to the edging of the garden (photograph: 1978).

Johnson Garden, Montecito, 1928–29. A view of that stately Monterey cypress in the English lawn. This garden, or room, has a green carpet of lawn and simple planting on both sides. It is often not how much you do, but how little you do that counts. The landscaping in this photograph is not fussy; it is simple and quiet (photograph: 1978).

Johnson Garden, Montecito, 1928–29. The south elevation of the Tuscan villa, taken from the extreme end of the south garden. This is framed by two tall, mature Monterey cypresses. All of the planting on the extreme right was done in 1929, from five-gallon cans. This mass planting creates a strong illusion. Anyone standing beside the photographer would never guess what was on the other side of this planting. Of such illusions is a garden created (photograph: 1978).

Johnson Garden, Montecito, 1928–29. Flora—removed from Mrs. Dan Murphy's garden in Los Angeles when that garden was destroyed. This is a good example of what just one statue can do for a garden. Flora is backlighted, and this photograph was taken late in the afternoon (photograph: 1978).

Johnson Garden, Montecito, 1928–29. A view of the north garden, photographed from the dining-room windows just after the planting was done. To me, the landscape architect, this is the epitome of what a garden should be—not because of what the landscape architect did, but because of the magnificent setting, the superb, dark green live oaks on either side, and the soft grey of the coast range in the background. Because the two low walls in the foreground interrupt the view, the walk seems longer. The fountain is the terminal of this view. It is in sunlight and is white against the dark green.

Johnson Garden, Montecito, 1928–29. The terminal fountain of the north garden; however, when you reach this fountain, you realize that it does not really terminate the garden, which goes on for another sixty feet, on a downhill slope (photograph: 1978).

Johnson Garden, Montecito, 1928–29. The pedestal of the fountain. Underneath the basin one can see the groove that forces the water to flow from the edge of the basin to the pool below, instead of dribbling down the underside of the basin (photograph: 1978).

Johnson Garden, Montecito, 1928–29. A view of the north gardens with the backdrop of mountains. It's our honor guard—a double row of citrus in terra-cotta pots on a cast-stone base. At the time of this photograph the plants had been in these pots for more than fifty years (photograph: 1978).

The Archibald Young Garden
Pasadena
1929

In the early fall of 1929, the Santa Barbara architect, George Washington Smith, was just completing an Andalusian home on the Arroyo Seco in Pasadena for Mr. and Mrs. Archibald Young. He recommended me to Mr. and Mrs. Young, and they retained me.

In the winter of 1927-28, Mrs. Hanson and I had gone to Europe for a month. We visited Seville and were overwhelmed with the gardens of the Maria Luisa Park. We also visited the Alhambra, the Generalife gardens at Granada, and the many small gardens in Cordova, which made a deep impression.

All these gardens used fountains—some large, some small. Many of them also had a tiny channel of water going down the middle of each path, something I had never seen before, which created a delightful atmosphere. The water running down the channels and the streams from the fountains added life to the gardens, besides having a cooling effect. All of these fountains and channels were of a scale that we could use in small gardens, even city-lot gardens, in Southern California. And I wondered why we had never used them.

While visiting George Washington Smith in Santa Barbara, I admired his own Spanish garden and alley of trees with a narrow channel of water running down the middle. I suggested to the Youngs that they, too, have an Andalusian garden. I made a layout which they approved, and I built the garden.

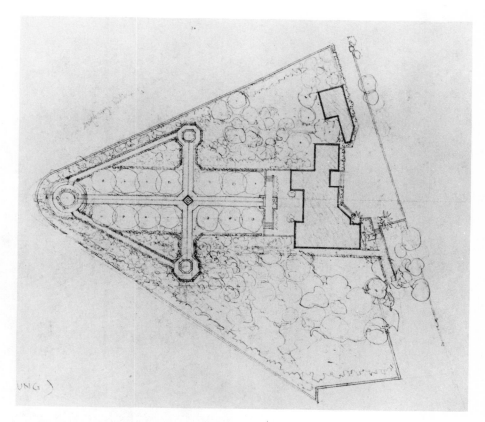

Young Garden, Pasadena, 1929. A recent sketch of the garden, by Leavitt Dudley, drawn by him with the landscape architect leaning over his shoulder, trying to remember what the garden was like fifty years before.

85

Young Garden, Pasadena, 1929. The house, by George Washington Smith, was Andalusian in character, a type of architecture certainly well suited to Southern California. The paving of cobblestones was miserable to walk on, but that's what the client wanted. A date palm ends the driveway, and the same type of foliage is echoed in the pots on the wall.

Young Garden, Pasadena, 1929. The auto court and the principal entrance to the house. On the left is a Strelitzia (bird of paradise), in the middle a fan palm, and on the right, bamboo. All different, all harmonious.

Young Garden, Pasadena, 1929. The intersection of the main alley and the crosswalk. A fine jet stream of water emanates from the small pool in the center of the intersection.

Young Garden, Pasadena, 1929. The start of the water channel. The source of the water is the lion's head. The material of the wall is rough concrete, with the grain and line of the board form showing. This garden contains more concrete and brick than plants, but the concrete and brick give form.

Young Garden, Pasadena, 1929. A view from the middle of the long alley. At this point there is a crosswalk. At the center of this intersection is a very low pool, with a glazed border tile from Guadalajara, Mexico. The planting is simplicity itself: low hedges of Texas privet, a strip of English ivy interplanted with olives. These trees were all moved in full-grown.

Young Garden, Pasadena, 1929. The terminal of the long alley.

*Left: Young Garden, Pasadena, 1929.
In the foreground is the start of the
crosswalk, and on the right the side of
a pool. There is a channel of water
down the center of this crosswalk.*

Young Garden, Pasadena, 1929. The terminal of the long alley was a circular bench.

Young Garden, Pasadena, 1929. Off to one side of the terminal were geometric formal gardens modeled, somewhat, from the gardens at the Generalife, Granada, Spain.

The Murphy Gardens
Los Angeles
1932

The Dan Murphy place was on the south side of West Adams, just to the west of Western Avenue. The house had been built for some time; the Murphys were either the second or third owners. It sat a considerable distance back from the street; had a huge, emerald green lawn; a curved, horseshoe, gravel-surfaced driveway; and a large expanse of land on either side of the house.

Mrs. Murphy had had three or four, maybe more, landscape architects work on her gardens. I don't think she was displeased with any of them. She was just hunting for fresh ideas. She was having a great deal of fun building gardens. The various gardens did not fit into a preconceived, overall plan. Her enjoyment was in creating them.

Although, like everyone in the landscape profession, I knew about Mrs. Murphy, I was much surprised to receive a telephone call from her in 1932. Things couldn't have been blacker for a landscape architect, although fortunately, I was no longer doing that work. I was doing land planning and land development. One of the reasons I thought Mrs. Murphy had called me was that she had probably run through her list of landscape architects.

I met with Mrs. Murphy; we got along. Although she was inclined to be tyrannical, her impeccable taste compensated for this.

She showed me a photograph of a small temple she had purchased in Italy, had dismantled and shipped to Los Angeles. Mrs. Murphy wanted to erect the temple and have it used as the focal point of a garden. She didn't know where. She just wanted an Italian garden, and she wanted to use that temple.

I told Mrs. Murphy that I hadn't had a landscape organization since Black October, 1929, but I would get hold of Lutah Maria Riggs, who could carry out my ideas. I would carry out Mrs. Murphy's ideas, and we'd have a good garden—one that she'd be proud of.

Murphy Garden, Los Angeles, 1932. The easiest way to describe the Dan Murphy gardens is that they were composed of a series of rooms. The Murphys' was an old estate, with many fine mature trees, a great help to the landscape architect. The trees really made the gardens. This is an octagonal garden, with a fine Italian piece— Diana, the Huntress—low, dark green Euonymus hedge, mass planting of various broad-leafed shrubs, and fine leaf shadows on the gravel. Beyond Diana, a path led into the round temple garden.

Murphy Garden, Los Angeles, 1932. The temple garden. The garden had four grass panels, with a round lily pool in the middle, an architectural curbing, good detail.

Murphy Garden, Los Angeles, 1932. This is close in spirit to a Maxfield Parrish painting of a garden. The view is framed twice; once with orange trees in terra-cotta pots, and the second time with the two big jars. The two pots and the jars, plus the hedging, interrupt your view and in doing so make the garden appear a great deal longer than it actually is.

I said Miss Riggs would be expensive and told Mrs. Murphy of Lutah Riggs's background and of her work on the Kirk B. Johnson estate. Mrs. Murphy and I went to Montecito to see the Kirk Johnson place, which was in perfect shape. Mrs. Murphy met Miss Riggs and liked her, and I was again in business as a landscape architect, but only for that one series of gardens. Miss Riggs, Mrs. Murphy, and all the rest of us had a ball for a year.

In my first conversation with Mrs. Murphy, I had told her I didn't know of anyone who had the expertise to put that temple back together again. Mrs. Murphy offhandedly said, ''I can get it erected. Mr. Murphy has a refrigeration corporation, and his head engineer can do anything. You tell me where you want the temple, and Mr. Murphy will see that his engineer erects it.'' And it was that simple. The engineer came out and visited with me. We liked each other; we got along. I don't know what Mr. Murphy thought of all this. I saw him a few times; he was very brusque and businesslike, but he never growled much about anything. However, he may have kicked some on the bills—they were getting pretty heavy.

With Lutah Riggs's help I designed a garden featuring the temple. When we were finished with that garden, which Mrs. Murphy liked, I had her walk with me over to a slope on which there was an avocado grove. I told Mrs. Murphy we could build a cascade down that slope. It would be in complete shadow, but at the bottom we could have a round pool with a piece of white statuary in the middle, and the pool and the statue would be in sunlight, making a lovely contrast with the shade of the cascade. I knew she'd like it and said I'd have Miss Riggs make some sketches. Miss Riggs made the sketches, and Mrs. Murphy did like them.

Mrs. Murphy was not afraid of doing something new. I explained to her that we would not have steps going down each side of the cascade, but rather a series of ramps, made of jet black, smooth pebbles. We built that cascade garden. Each of the basins was carved out of solid stone. Mrs. Murphy had acquired the olive jars used on either side of the cascade path in Italy. She had never seen anything like our cascade in Italy, but I had at the Villa d'Este at Bellagio on Lake Como, and I had taken a number of photographs of its cascade, which I showed Miss Riggs.

One day Mrs. Murphy showed me a photograph of another temple that was stored in crates on the property. The photograph was of a beautiful little thing; the dome was filigreed ironwork. I told Mrs. Murphy that I had just the spot for that temple. Again, I had Miss Riggs make a bird's-eye sketch of that garden. She and I had drawn the garden ideas out of our heads, with the help of photographs and strong cups of coffee and doughnuts—which is part of the standard diet of garden architects. Mrs. Murphy said, ''Well, that's delightful. We'll do it.'' And we did.

Mrs. Murphy's friend, and now my friend, the refrigeration engineer, erected the temple. He was an expert craftsman. We built the garden, which was composed of a gravel path lined with an edging of split brick, *Pittosporum* hedges, and an alley of olive trees. I always loved that garden. Mrs. Murphy was a perfectionist. She objected to the look of the brand new split brick. I solved that problem for her by hauling in a big truckload of fresh cow manure. We dug up our brand new split bricks and buried them in the manure,

Murphy Garden, Los Angeles, 1932. Opposite view of the temple garden. A thin jet of water emanates from the lily pool. The garden ends with a thin, white marble piece of statuary.

and they were satisfactorily toned down. Mrs. Murphy liked them.

Then she presented me with another problem—which I couldn't solve. She didn't like the stark white color of the high retaining wall for this temple garden. One day she said to me, ''Mr. Hanson, tomorrow we're going to drive to the old mission in Ventura. I want to show you the color that I want that wall to be.'' We drove to Ventura, and I saw the mission and the color of its wall. My heart sank, because the mission wall had been painted and repainted many times over the past 175 years—all kinds of different shades, depending on the taste of the priest in charge at the time. The dust and what-have-you would accumulate on the wall, and it would be repainted again. It had patina. I told Mrs. Murphy that only time would make her wall the way she visualized it. And she was satisfied.

We had run out of room; the party was over. Miss Riggs went back to Santa Barbara to practice architecture, and I went about my business of developing land.

I cannot be thankful enough to Mrs. Murphy for all she unknowingly taught me, and I know that she got a great deal of enjoyment from finger-pointing at me. And Mr. Murphy did not mind paying the bills. He, too, had oil wells.

Left: Murphy Garden, Los Angeles, 1932. A view of the beginning of the cascade. Lutah Maria Riggs designed the urn on the right, as well as the balustrade. It was all of solid stone. The cascade was of Tuffa stone. All of the walks were paved with black pebbles, picked up on the seacoast between Los Angeles and San Diego.

Murphy Garden, Los Angeles, 1932. This is the cascade in the middle of an avocado orchard. The foreground is interrupted with a balustrade, which gives distance. Then the series of cascade basins slopes downhill. A number of parallel lines going downhill give a perspective. Sometimes landscape architects and architects fake the perspective. I don't think it's ever necessary. The cascade terminates at a round pool with a piece of statuary in its center. The terminal is in sunlight, with a background of dark foliage.

Right: Murphy Garden, Los Angeles, 1932. The end of the cascade, a duplicate of one at the Villa d'Este, Bellagio, Lake Como, Italy.

Murphy Garden, Los Angeles, 1932. The bottom of the cascade.

Murphy Garden, Los Angeles, 1932. Looking from the terminal fountain to the beginning of the cascade.

Right: Murphy Garden, Los Angeles, 1932. The pattern of the pebble landing.

Murphy Garden, Los Angeles, 1932. The parapet wall provides good, strong architecture. Plain, simple, restrained—double stairway, bottom landing of pebble mosaic, a shell niche with Flora inside. We called this garden the "olive-walk" garden.

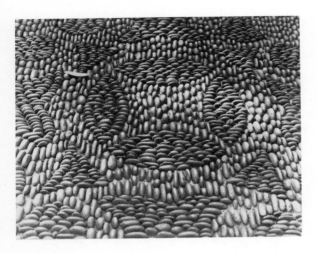

Murphy Garden, Los Angeles, 1932. The floor of the temple in the ''olive-walk'' garden.

Murphy Garden, Los Angeles, 1932. A close-up of the terminal. One can see the pattern of the mosaic pebble work.

98

Murphy Garden, Los Angeles, 1932. One of the landscape architect's favorite photographs. A satisfactory garden. The background, the terminal, is the other beautiful little temple that Mrs. Murphy had stored in crates in a shed on the estate. The garden comprises that temple, a gravel path with split-brick edging, a number of fully grown, low-branched olive trees, and a ground cover of ivy. The right-hand wall of the garden is of dark green, broad-leafed evergreen shrubs, untrimmed. The left-hand edge of the garden is a complete contrast—it's garden architecture—a plain, simple, parapet wall.

Index